MYSTERIES OF THE DEAD SEA SCROLLS

Harvey Minkoff, Ph.D.

HALO PRESS

MYSTERIES OF THE
DEAD SEA
SCROLLS

Harvey Minkoff, Ph.D.

Cover photo montage by Susan Chamberlain
[for jars] SuperStock
[for map] A.K.G. Berlin/SuperStock

Table of Contents

JERICHO

JERUSALEM

BETHLEHEM

QUMRAN

EIN FESHKHA

KHIRBET
MIRD

R. Jordan

*Wadi
Murabba'at*

𝔇ead
𝔖ea

EIN GEDI

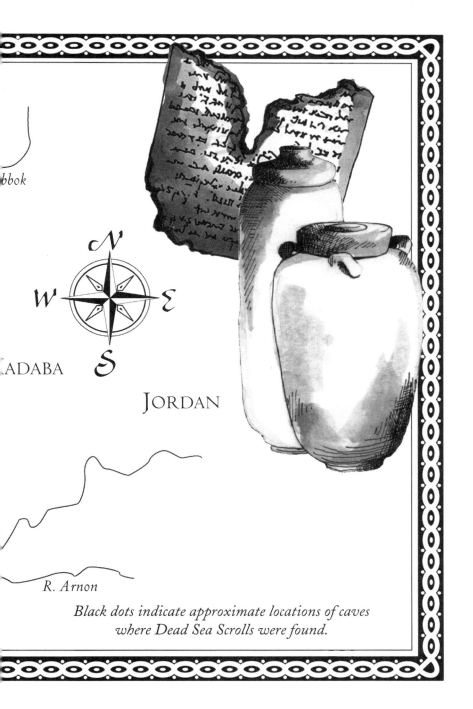

bbok

ADABA

JORDAN

R. Arnon

Black dots indicate approximate locations of caves
where Dead Sea Scrolls were found.

Introduction

Heroes. Villains. Ancient treasures. Smugglers. Coded messages. Secret meetings. Anonymous buyers. The true story of the Dead Sea Scrolls, set in the war-torn Middle East, is the stuff of a Hollywood thriller.

The most important manuscript find of the twentieth century—the discovery of the Dead Sea Scrolls in 1947—began with a shepherd boy's search for one of his goats among the limestone cliffs of southern Palestine, now a part of Israel. Or perhaps it didn't. Because the removal of the scrolls from the cave and the attempt to sell them privately were both illegal, the tribesmen and dealers who tried to sell the scrolls told almost everybody a different story about when, how, and where the scrolls had been found. By the time soldiers and religious experts discovered the location of the scrolls, many of the sites had been looted rather than properly dug up. Consequently, the true story of how this historic archaeological treasure was found is covered in mystery.

The story of who came to own the scrolls is just as dramatic as their discovery. Because of the war between Arabs and Jews, travel in Palestine was difficult; danger was everywhere. Friends risked their lives to meet at the barbed wire barricades that separated Arab from Jew in Jerusalem. Because of this situation, experts who could have identified the scrolls' true value could not be reached. People living only a mile apart could not discuss what they had seen. In addition, there were fights over who should control the scrolls. Jews felt that the scrolls belonged to them. Christians believed that their own claim was superior. Anonymous buyers and overseas meetings finally resolved some of these conflicts.

The first investigation of the scrolls was marked by both great achievement and missed opportunities. Tens of thousands of pieces of the scrolls were sorted, matched, and assembled by a small team of dedicated experts who completed their backbreaking work in an amazingly short time. However, when the time came to figure out what the scrolls said, confusion reigned. This was partly because although the scrolls dealt with Jewish law from a period of great importance to Judaism, the assembly team contained no Jewish scholars. Instead, the Christian editors, many of them Catholic clergymen, found predictions about the Christian world, which led to many misinterpretations of what the scrolls were really about.

The clergymen were particularly interested in descriptions of the Teacher of Righteousness, who dominates some of the scrolls. Was he the leader of an ancient cult—perhaps the Messiah himself? And what about the Wicked Priest? Reports that in the scrolls the Wicked Priest crucified the Teacher of Righteousness rocked the Christian world because the story had obvious similarities to the life of Jesus. Were the scrolls written by Christians, or was the Gospel a story modeled on the scrolls? It turned out that the scroll in question was actually not very clear, and the editor's interpretation contained more made-up stories than actual fact.

There were many more questions than answers about the content of the scrolls, because so much important information was withheld from other experts as well as from the public. Because the original investigative team kept the scrolls to itself, the discovery of the century became one of the great scandals of modern scholarship. When they were discovered, the scrolls caused excitement throughout the world but then were virtually forgotten by the public for almost forty years. Was the original excitement caused merely by a lot of media attention, or did the loss of interest result from a plot? The first reports on the scrolls promised new information about Jesus and early Christianity. Did people lose interest when what was revealed seemed limited to Judaism? Or was the new information so explosive that it led to a cover-up? Conspiracy theories began to surface.

Many other questions surround the Dead Sea scrolls. Who wrote them and when? Why were they hidden in caves near the Dead Sea? When were they found and by whom? And why, after fifty years, do so many mysteries still remain?

The following pages offer answers to these questions and many more. Here you will find the real-life drama of how a chance discovery launched a history-making search into the mysteries of the Dead Sea Scrolls.

CHAPTER 1

Smugglers, Soldiers, Scrolls

Some people called it smuggling. But to the local tribesmen, the Ta'amireh Bedouin in the Holy Land, moving merchandise from Transjordan (now known as Jordan) to Jericho and on to Bethlehem was a way of life. The Ta'amireh had lived in the rocky desert of the Palestinian wilderness for 300 years— grazing their flocks in the dusty canyons, wandering over the unmapped trails between towering limestone cliffs, exploring the caves and gullies carved by ancient waters running down to the Dead Sea. Why should these desert dwellers care whether the distant government was called the Ottoman Empire, a British territory, or Transjordan? Boundaries drawn on a map meant nothing to them.

But to others—to merchants, clergy, religious experts, and museum officials—laws and boundaries *did* mean something. In addition, documents such as receipts, bills, and invoices were all part of the antiquities (ancient objects) trade, and they, too, were important. Unfortunately, because there are no such documents on the Dead Sea Scrolls, their discovery remains clouded by lies, double-talk, and conflicting stories.

How were the Dead Sea Scrolls discovered? According to one popular telling of the story, in the spring of 1947 a young

Bedouin shepherd named Muhammad—nicknamed edh-Dhib, or "the wolf"—was tending the family goats a mile or so north of a freshwater spring called Ein Feshkha at the northwest tip of the Dead Sea. When a goat scampered up the steep slopes, the boy followed. Unable to locate the animal, and worn out by the difficult climb in the hot desert afternoon, the boy sat down in the shade of a rock. In an attempt to get the goat to come out of a possible hiding place, he threw a stone through the small opening of a cave he had seen high overhead.

But instead of the hollow ring of stone on stone, he heard the crashing of pottery. He climbed as near as he could to the cave and, hanging by his fingertips, pulled himself up to look into the darkness. He dimly made out a row of clay jars, each about two or three feet tall.

Convinced that only demons and imps could live in a cave whose tiny opening hung so high in a cliff, the boy dropped to the ground and ran away. That night, back in the camp, he told his older cousin about what he had seen. The two agreed that the demons who hid the treasure in the cave were certainly long gone and that they could safely return to claim it.

Two days later they climbed to the cave, some 350 feet up the slope, and slithered into it. After prying open several jars, they at last found one that contained several bundles of rags wrapped around foul-smelling objects covered in a sticky, tar-like substance. They looked more closely and saw that the objects were rolls of fragile leather. Not knowing what they held in their hands, the two boys took the rolls back to their camp, where they shoved them into a sack. There the rolls stayed for several months. Then one day, the boys happened to show their discovery to an antiquities dealer who happened to be a Christian and whose parish priest happened to be a collector of ancient writings. In this way, after many comical twists and turns, the first Dead Sea Scrolls came to light.

In other versions of the discovery, the date was November or December 1946; the boy was a teenager or a young man; he was looking for sheep or a goat; he was accompanied by one or two adult cousins; he threw the rock out of boredom or to check caves for wild animals; and he may not have been Muhammad edh-Dhib but his cousin Juma'a Muhammad Khalil. Yet all versions of the story have one thing in common: they portray the discovery as the romantic tale of an innocent shepherd boy who happened by pure chance onto the archaeological find of the century. Such a tale of innocent luck would certainly have served the purpose of the Ta'amireh Bedouin if they were, in fact, smugglers and looters.

Another theory is that the Bedouin were only playing with their audience. In *Solving the Mysteries of the Dead Sea Scrolls*, Edward M. Cook explains that conflicting versions of the discovery may have surfaced because Muhammad and his friends "may have amused themselves by telling a different tale to every earnest Westerner who asked them." Like many uneducated but not unwise "locals" who feel that outsiders treat them with disrespect, they may have been weaving a tale worthy of *Arabian Nights* simply to outfox the Western world.

Other authors believe that the Ta'amireh Bedouin told this story to cover their illegal activities. Neil Asher Silberman, in *The Hidden Scrolls*, describes the Ta'amireh as cunning traders, with a talent for finding and selling antiquities. According to him, Juma'a was "an experienced hunter for antiquities," who "knew exactly what he was looking for" when he threw that rock into the cave. It seems that the Taʿamireh had for many years been working with respected archaeologists and were "far more skillful, thorough, and daring" in locating artifacts—objects made by humans in ancient times—than the so-called experts who looked down on them.

Members of the tribe had worked in archaeological digs near Bethlehem, where they learned techniques they later used in their own illegal explorations. In some cases, Silberman says, they even sold artifacts from these secret digs to their employers at official locations. In terms of their trading savvy, he concludes, these Bedouin should be considered not scavengers but crafty businessmen. But perhaps Silberman's most amazing report is what was going on as much as a decade before the "discovery" of the Dead Sea Scrolls: The Bedouin were selling ancient coins to Jewish workers at a chemical plant near the Dead Sea and offering to show them caves with "books from the time of your kings!"

John Allegro, one of the original members of the international editorial team, treats the Bedouin less kindly. In *The Dead Sea Scrolls: A Reappraisal*, he says straight out that the Taʿamireh were smugglers and sometimes highwaymen. His account is filled with contempt both for the Taʿamireh and for the respectable citizens who later launched their own illegal and destructive excavations.

As we will see in the next chapter, although the shepherds and their middlemen had to overcome many obstacles to sell the scrolls to cautious experts, the value of the scrolls eventually became clear. The Bedouin had found three scrolls, which they entrusted to a shoemaker and part-time antiquities dealer named Khalil Iskander (Kando) Shahin. Kando sold them to

Athanasius Yeshue Samuel, or Mar ("Master" or "Father") Samuel, the Syrian Orthodox metropolitan (the equivalent of a Western bishop) of Jerusalem.

But even as Kando made this deal, he and an associate, George Isaiah (Shaya or Ishaya in Arabic), returned to the cave and discovered four more scrolls, along with a number of scroll fragments. Shortly afterward, Mar Samuel sent his own men to the cave and, as Allegro explains, did a lot of harm to the area. Wanting only the manuscripts, these scavengers carelessly threw linen wrappings and broken pottery into a mound outside, destroying priceless archaeological information. The looting went on for more than a year, apparently until August 1948. During this time respected experts were kept from the caves. The Bedouin were determined to protect their treasure.

To make matters worse, the Holy Land at that time was in a state of war and great confusion. After the collapse of the Ottoman Empire in World War I, the League of Nations established what was called the British Mandate in Palestine—in other words, Britain had administrative control of the area. Unfortunately, the policy of the British toward the Holy Land changed constantly, leading to more tension between Arabs and Jews in the area. First the British supported a Jewish homeland in Palestine and then, bowing to Arab opposition, they restricted Jewish immigration there.

In 1927, the British separated the large area east of the Jordan River to create Transjordan. In the rest of the British Mandate, throughout the 1920s and 1930s, fighting between Arabs and Jews was common and often bloody. During World War II, the Jews of Palestine formed a military unit in the British army, while many Palestinian Arabs supported the

Germans on the grounds that their enemy's enemy was their friend. After the war, illegal Jewish immigration into Palestine increased, as those who escaped the Nazi death camps looked for a safe place in the promised homeland. The British, caught in the struggle between the two communities under their rule, looked for a way to get themselves out of Palestine completely.

It was during this time of great confusion and unrest that the Dead Sea Scrolls were found. Kando, the antiquities dealer, was trying to sell the scrolls during the summer and fall of 1947, just as the United Nations voted to divide Palestine into two states. As the British prepared to end their administration, riots, bombings, and sniping tore apart everyday life throughout Palestine, especially in major cities like Jerusalem. Both Arabs and Jews suffered many casualties; both sides were getting ready for an inevitable war. The day after the establishment of the state of Israel on May 14, 1948, it was invaded by the armies of Egypt, Syria, Transjordan, Lebanon, and Iraq. When the fighting ended with a cease-fire in early 1949, Jerusalem was divided into Arab and Jewish sections. The American and French archaeological schools, St. Mark's Monastery, and the Palestine Archaeological Museum were all in the Arab sector. Transjordan occupied the area on the West Bank of the Jordan River that included the cave of the scrolls.

Mar Samuel took the scrolls to Beirut for safekeeping during the fighting, and the experts at the American Schools of Oriental Research left Jerusalem for the United States. There, the organization's office at Yale University put out a statement about the scrolls on April 11, 1948, saying that the "earliest known manuscript" of Isaiah had been "found in the Syrian monastery of St. Mark in Jerusalem" and had been recently identified by members of the American Schools. The news release also mentioned three other scrolls: a commentary on the biblical book of Habakkuk, a "manual of discipline" for a Jewish sect (a special group of believers), and text that was later identified and labeled the Genesis Apocryphon.

On April 25, the *New York Times* reported that ancient scrolls had been found in a cave near an ancient settlement called Ein Gedi, some miles down the western shore of the Dead Sea. The following day, Professor Eliezer Sukenik, founder of the Institute for Archaeology at the Hebrew University in Jerusalem, confirmed that he had three scrolls: a partial manuscript of Isaiah, a collection of hymns, and a work about the final war between the forces of Good and Evil. Also in April, the *Bulletin of the American Schools of Oriental Research* announced that ancient scrolls being studied at the American Schools and at the Hebrew University would "revolutionize" biblical studies.

But because of the fighting in the Middle East, none of this news came to the attention of G. Lankester Harding, director of the Jordanian Department of Antiquities, until the following November, a year and a half after the first scrolls were found.

Harding—the picture of an English colonial official— immediately ordered Joseph Sa'ad, secretary of the Palestine Museum in Jerusalem, to find the cave. At St. Mark's, Sa'ad interviewed an uncooperative George Isaiah and an elderly priest, Father Yusif, who had been sent by Mar Samuel to confirm that the cave existed. Father Yusif told Harding and Sa'ad the general location of the cave: south of the Jericho road, west of the Dead Sea.

These directions were pathetically inadequate. For centuries, caves in this forbidding countryside provided hiding places for both people and property. Finding these caves, much less one particular cave, was extremely difficult. Rain frequently weakened the limestone and caused the roofs of the caves to collapse. Even worse, the area experienced earthquakes that reshaped the land, burying or concealing the caves. Sa'ad knew that he would need more precise directions to find the cave, and he offered to hire George Isaiah, Kando's friend, as a guide and pay him a percentage of everything he discovered. But after several weeks of negotiation, Isaiah abruptly backed out.

Thereafter, either through the help of Captain Philippe Lippens, a Belgian serving as a United Nations observer, or through a chance meeting with soldiers of the Jordanian Arab Legion, Harding and Sa'ad came up with a plan to have these desert warriors scout the area described by Father Yusif. With the approval of the British commander of the Arab Legion, troops were sent to the area under an English brigadier and a Jordanian captain. The soldiers started at the Jericho road and proceeded southward, shoulder to shoulder so that all the slopes and cliffs could be scanned. Harding waited anxiously for news of their search.

Three days later, at the end of January 1949, the soldiers found the cave of the scrolls. Harding eagerly joined them and decided that a full-scale excavation should begin. The digging took place from February 15 to March 5, 1949, and it included Harding, Sa'ad, and Father Roland de Vaux of the École Biblique. The diggings unearthed dozens of scroll fragments and pieces of linen and pottery, similar to those found by the Bedouin. The archaeologists estimated that the wreckage they found represented between forty and fifty jars, from which they guessed that more than a hundred scrolls might have been in the original group. The scrolls held by Mar Samuel and the Hebrew University accounted for seven. Where were the rest of them?

The missing scrolls now had to be tracked down. This would not be easy, of course, for whoever had the scrolls knew they were carrying illegal material and might be arrested. But Harding was more interested in gathering the manuscripts for study than in prosecuting anyone, so he authorized Sa'ad to pay up to £1 (about $4) per square centimeter of text fragment. By liberally spreading around bribes and promises of much more money to come, Harding and Sa'ad were led back to our old friend Kando, the antiquities dealer, and through him to the Ta'amireh Bedouin, who eventually revealed the details that the archaeologists needed.

After Harding and Sa'ad paid Kando £1,000 for the fragments he was selling, scroll hunting seems to have become the main business of the Ta'amireh. No longer afraid of the authorities, the Bedouin continued their illegal excavations, in a sense competing with the official digs. In October 1951, they excavated another cave, and soon Sa'ad was visited at his museum by Bedouin offering to sell additional scroll fragments. Although he expressed interest, the sellers did not appear at the appointed time. Sa'ad once again asked for help from the army and was given a few men, a jeep, and a letter of authorization for his search.

When Sa'ad and his escort found one of the Bedouin who had visited the museum, they forced him to take them to the cave, which turned out to be in Wadi Murabba'at, about ten miles south of Qumran on the western shore of the Dead Sea. There, much to their amazement, they encountered a group of Bedouin excavating a huge cave more than 10 feet high, 20 feet wide, and 150 feet long.

The soldiers searched the Bedouin but found no illegal material on them and released them. This expedition proved to be a public relations nightmare for Sa'ad and the army: They were accused of kidnapping a citizen walking peacefully in the street, detaining and bullying workers, and using abusive military power against civilians. But eventually documents from the Murabba'at caves surfaced in the antiquities market and were bought at the established price. In addition to some fragments dating to the seventh or eighth centuries B.C., during the reign of the kings of Judah, and some dating to the much later Arab period, the find contained biblical material that experts would usefully compare to similar texts from the area near Qumran. Most exciting, the cave held letters from Bar-Kokhba, a Jewish leader who had led a bitter revolt in 135 A.D. against the Romans, who had conquered Jerusalem about sixty years earlier. Bar-Kokhba had operated from these mountains during their revolt.

Between November 24 and December 12, 1951, Harding and de Vaux conducted an investigation of Khirbet ("ruin of") Qumran. This ancient settlement, identified as an unimportant Roman fort, was less than a mile south of the cave where the first scrolls were found. Harding and de Vaux found no written material at the site, but they did unearth pottery similar to that in the cave and thus were able to make a connection between the two sites.

Harding then moved on to Wadi Murabba'at, where in

January 1952 he supervised an official dig at four caves, with the paid assistance of some of the Bedouin who had been excavating there illegally four months earlier. In February 1952, less than two months after Harding had left Qumran, the Bedouin discovered a second cave near there and dug up thirty-three manuscript fragments. Understandably embarrassed at missing the site, the professionals decided to begin a complete survey of the area. During March 1952, experts from the American and French schools examined more than 200 caves and hiding places along a five-mile stretch of the Dead Sea. On March 14, they discovered another scroll cave, half a mile north of Cave 1. Called Cave 3, it contained fourteen manuscripts, a large number of jars and jugs, and the Copper Scroll, a mysterious script written on sheets of copper.

In July and August of 1952, the Bedouin unearthed more manuscripts at Khirbet Mird and at a second site and sold them to the Jordanian Department of Antiquities. The material from Khirbet Mird was Christian from the fifth century or later and therefore was unrelated to the other finds. However, documents from the second site dated to the period when Bar-Kokhba was leading his struggle against the Romans. According to Yigael Yadin in his book *Bar-Kokhba*, Yadin's father, the Hebrew University's Professor Sukenik, had long been planning a full-scale exploration of the wilderness on Israel's side of the border, especially around the settlement of Ein Gedi. But ill health had stopped him. Now this news from Jordan made it clear that the Bedouin were smuggling Jewish antiquities out of Israel into Jordan. A team of searchers from the Israeli Department of Antiquities was quickly put together. They searched the settlement of Nahal

Hever from November 25 to December 16, 1953, and found that the site had been looted. But they were able to recover bits of pottery, cloth, and mats from the time of the Jewish rebel Bar-Kokhba and enough evidence in the form of Jordanian cigarette boxes and the like to prove that the Bedouin had been at work there.

In August 1952, a Bedouin expedition discovered a fourth cave at Qumran, yet another site that Harding's team had missed. As usual, it is impossible to know whether the Bedouin were telling the truth or spinning a tale, but they claimed that they discovered this cave, too, by following an animal. According to an oft-repeated story, an old Bedouin tribesman, perhaps having heard the young men talk about their excavations, was reminded that years before he had been hunting partridge in the hills behind the ruins at Qumran. One wounded bird struggled into a crack in the rocky hillside. When the hunter followed, he discovered a hollowed-out cave with holes carved into the walls. In one of them he found an ancient lamp. Since that time he had given no thought to the incident, but now, hearing about the scroll discoveries of the Bedouin, he thought that perhaps his kinsmen might want to look for that cave.

The most dramatic materials were found in Cave 4. Deliberately carved into the limestone hillside, the cave contained two rooms connected to an oval chamber. Holes in the walls had once held wooden shelves on which more than 500 scrolls had been neatly stored—books of the Bible, selections from the Apocrypha (books written after the Old Testament that are included in some versions of the Bible but not in others), previously unknown sectarian literature (containing special rituals or beliefs of a separate Jewish group of believers), and other works. This was not a hiding place but an actual library, possibly belonging to the people who lived at Qumran, several minutes' walk to the east. The Bedouin removed about 15,000 manuscript fragments from Cave 4 and lied about the source when they tried to sell them. Somehow Harding learned the truth, and when he and Father Roland de Vaux examined the cave at the end of September 1952, they unearthed additional fragments. Even forty years later, much of this vast treasure remained a secret.

Archaeologists working in Cave 4 discovered Cave 5 just to the north, while Bedouin found Cave 6 to the west. Each of these caves contained fragments of about twenty-five or thirty manuscripts. In February and April of 1955, archaeologists at the Qumran ruins discovered four more caves slightly south of the ruins and east of Cave 4. The manuscript findings from these locations were small: one piece of papyrus (an ancient form of paper) in Cave 9, one piece of pottery in Cave 10, five fragments of text in Cave 8, and nineteen or so fragments from Cave 7.

Then, in January 1956, the Bedouin found another important cave up in the cliffs between Caves 1 and 3. This one, numbered 11, had apparently been examined earlier by archaeologists, who thought it was empty. But when the Bedouin had their turn, they discovered that the rear wall of the cave was actually a collapsed roof. Behind this pile of rock they found a scooped-out secret place with a neatly stored pile of twenty-one manuscripts, some in very good condition.

Later in 1956, the Middle East heated up again. After overthrowing King Farouk of Egypt, Gamal Abdel Nasser launched his pan-Arab movement—an attempt to unite all Arabs against outside rule—with its program for removing Western colonial influence. When Nasser seized control of the Suez Canal, Egypt was attacked in October 1956 by forces from Britain, France, and Israel. Although Nasser's army was quickly humiliated, he triumphed when the United Nations ordered the invaders to withdraw. Jordan was swept by Arab pride and removed many of the foreigners in its government, including the British head of the Arab Legion and Lankester Harding, who had been so committed to the collection of the Dead Sea Scrolls.

In March-April of 1960, the Israelis conducted a major exploration of the western shore of the Dead Sea, from the border with Jordan southward about 10 miles. The area was divided into four zones, each with its own team. The picked-over zone of Nahal Hever and its surroundings was assigned to Yigael Yadin. This time, with the assistance of helicopters, army trucks, and portable generators, his team discovered an important collection of written material from the Bar-Kokhba rebellion: biblical texts, administrative letters, and commercial documents. From October 1963 to May 1964 and from November 1964 to April 1965, Yadin led yet another excavation at Masada, a 1,300-foot-high mountain some twenty miles south of Qumran on the western shore of the Dead Sea. On the flat, oval-shaped top of the mountain, King Herod had built a palace fortress, which a hundred years later was the site of the last stand of the Jewish rebels in the first war against Rome. This excavation also uncovered some important texts.

Scroll fragments continued to surface for many years. Perhaps they really were discovered long after the first scrolls were found, or perhaps their holders were cleverly releasing them slowly to increase their value. After Israel gained possession of the Qumran area as a result of the Six Day War in 1967, it took charge of the official searches. In November of 1993, the Israelis conducted Operation Scroll. Three hundred volunteers divided into twenty teams to explore hundreds of caves. In January 1996, twenty volunteers examined six more caves near Qumran.

But the biggest discoveries had already been made four decades earlier. The Bedouin and, to a lesser degree, the professional archaeologists, had brought to light tens of thousands of scroll fragments. Who would own them? What would be done with them?

CHAPTER 2

Coded Messages and Anonymous Buyers

If the discovery of the Dead Sea Scrolls is a cloak-and-dagger tale, the story of what happened to them afterward is equally so, spiced with both unlikely comedy and deep mystery. This second story also introduces the unhappy mix of religion and politics that had disastrous consequences for a clear under-standing of the scrolls.

After the first scrolls had hung for months in a sack on a tent pole in the Ta'amireh Bedouin camp, the two boys who discovered them took the scrolls to Bethlehem. They first went to an antiquities dealer named Ibrahim Ijha, who feared that the merchandise was illegal. Then they went to Kando, who gave the Bedouin £5, about $20, and agreed to try to sell the scrolls for a one-third commission.

Kando and his friend George Isaiah belonged to the Syrian Orthodox Church and suspected that the strange writ-ing on the leather might be Syriac, an ancient form of Syrian writing. On a visit to Jerusalem during Holy Week 1947, one of them mentioned the scrolls to Mar Samuel of St. Mark's Monastery, which supposedly is the site of the Last Supper. St. Mark's had a large collection of old manuscripts in its library, and Mar Samuel himself was something of an expert on ancient writings, although some accounts say he was a mere dabbler in the field. He asked to see the scrolls and recognized the writing as ancient Hebrew. He also broke off a small piece of a scroll and burned it to see if the material was leather. Convinced that the scrolls were of interest, and perhaps of value, he offered to buy them.

Mar Samuel, Kando, the Bedouin—everyone involved, in fact—knew that this dealing in unauthorized excavations and antiquities was illegal. Their attempts to disguise their activities read like a comedy of errors. For example, Kando buried one or more of the scrolls in his garden. Unfortunately, this moist soil was not the dry dust of a desert cave, and when he dug up his treasure, it was a mass of smelly, sticky tar. The Bedouin had more scrolls, and Kando called Mar Samuel again in July to arrange a meeting. Kando's associate, George Isaiah, failed to show up at the appointed time, and Mar Samuel went about his business. When Samuel happened to mention the missed meeting to one of his colleagues, he was told that three suspicious-looking Arabs (Isaiah and his Bedouin accomplices) had asked for him earlier in the day, and, of course, had not been admitted. Mar Samuel telephoned Kando and tried to restart the negotiations.

According to one version of the story, after they had been turned away, George Isaiah and the angry Bedouin tribesmen met a Jewish merchant on their way back to Bethlehem. The merchant offered to buy the scrolls if the three would accompany him to his office where he had sufficient cash. But Isaiah resisted, either because he was loyal to Mar Samuel or because he feared a plot to lure them to the Jewish sector where they might be robbed. In another version, the Bedouin decided to improve their chances of a sale by giving part of their merchandise to another antiquities dealer, Faidi Salahi. In any event, by August, goodwill prevailed among men, and Mar Samuel had bought five scrolls (two of which turned out to be parts of the same manuscript) for about $100 or, some say, his life savings of $250.

Mar Samuel now tried to figure out exactly what he had bought. He asked experts in Jerusalem for their opinions about the age and authenticity of the scrolls and all had conflicting responses. Stephen Hanna Stephen, a minor official of the Palestine Department of Antiquities, believed that the story about finding ancient scrolls in a cave was too fantastic to be true, and he even refused to pass the information on to a superior for fear of looking foolish. Next, Mar Samuel showed the scrolls to a Syrian Orthodox priest at the École Biblique, the French biblical and archaeological school. The priest in turn introduced Mar Samuel to a young Dutch Dominican named J. van der Ploeg from the University of Nijmegen, who was studying at the school that year. Van der Ploeg recognized one of the scrolls as the biblical book of Isaiah, but could not offer an opinion about its age. An older priest who had lived in the Middle East for many years suggested caution because he knew there was a thriving business in phony religious objects. Two librarians from the Hebrew University were invited to St. Mark's; they declared the writing to be Samaritan, an ancient Hebrew alphabet.

In 1955, Edmund Wilson published *The Scrolls from the Dead Sea*, one of the first books to fire the public's imagination about the scrolls. Wilson wondered why someone of Mar Samuel's stature could not immediately find a competent, first-rate scholar to examine the scrolls. He blames the mis-trust between competing ethnic and religious groups. Arabs did not trust Jews, Christians did not deal with Muslims, and even the different denominations of Christians did not coop-erate with each other. Kando, a Syrian Christian, showed the scrolls to the Syrian metropolitan, Mar Samuel, who sought advice from members of his congregation. But the advice they received was inadequate, and so they turned to other Christians and eventually, and reluctantly, to Jews.

In November 1947, Faidi Salahi, the antiquities dealer, contacted Eliezer Sukenik, a professor at the Hebrew University. An ardent supporter of Israel, Sukenik had emi-grated in 1912 from Poland to Palestine, where he pioneered the study of Jewish archaeology. He had excavated ancient synagogues and tombs and knew a lot about the history of Hebrew scripts. Despite the violence threatening to engulf the country and the barbed wire that the British hoped would keep the Arabs and Jews of Jerusalem apart, the two men met. Salahi produced a piece of parchment covered with writing. Sukenik immediately recognized the writing as similar to writ-ings on tombs from the first century. But he had only seen this kind of writing carved or painted on stone, never on leather. It was possible that the parchment was a fake, but it was not likely, because of the uniqueness of the material. Sukenik asked to see more samples. The next day the two men met again, and Professor Eliezer Sukenik offered to buy all the fragments Salahi owned.

At the time, the United Nations was preparing to vote on the division of Palestine into Jewish and Arab states. Sukenik's son Yigael—who, as an officer in the Jewish underground army, had adopted the Hebrew surname Yadin, or "he will judge"—insisted that a trip into the Arab section was too dangerous. The Arabs opposed the plan to divide Palestine, and, win or lose, violence was certain. Nonetheless, Sukenik took the bus to Bethlehem. The tall, stocky Eastern European Jew must have been very noticeable on a bus filled with Arabs, but he returned safely with two scrolls and two of the storage jars. That evening he heard that the United Nations had approved the establishment of a Jewish state, Israel. Jews celebrated. Arabs rioted. Sukenik divided his time between celebrating and studying the fragments. His son, Yigael Yadin, would later write in *The Message of the Scrolls*:

> "I cannot avoid the feeling that there is something symbolic in the discovery of the scrolls and their acquisition at the moment of the creation of the State of Israel. It is as if these manuscripts had been waiting in caves for two thousand years...until the people of Israel had returned to their home and regained their freedom."

Two days after acquiring the scrolls, Sukenik wrote in his diary: "It may be that this is one of the greatest finds ever made in Palestine, a find we never so much as hoped for." Unable to travel because of the violence, he wrote: "I'm bursting to know what will come of it all. It might turn out that the neighborhood has many things of this sort. Who knows what surprises still await us." At the end of December he was again able to meet Salahi and at this time bought a third scroll.

More surprises awaited him. Because of the unrest in the country and the desire of the Bedouin to keep their activities secret, Sukenik and Mar Samuel did not know of each other's involvement with the scrolls. Anton Kiraz, a parishioner of St. Mark's, had once given Sukenik permission to dig up an ancient tomb on his property. In January 1948, he asked Sukenik to look at some scrolls from St. Mark's. Sukenik saw immediately that they were similar to those he had recently received from Salahi. Sukenik offered Kiraz £100 for the scrolls, then £500, and finally £1,000. Kiraz said that the deal was up to Mar Samuel, but he did allow Sukenik to study one of the scrolls, a copy of Isaiah, for a week.

In February 1948, Mar Samuel's colleague and longtime friend Butros Sowmy entered the picture. He apparently urged Mar Samuel not to sell such valuable items to a Jew. Instead, because Sowmy had previously dealt with the American Schools of Oriental Research in Jerusalem, he now asked experts there to help identify and date some scrolls that had been found in the library of St. Mark's. After comparing them with photographs in the research library at the American Schools, John Trever, William Brownlee, and the school's director, Millar Burrows, decided that the scrolls were indeed very old, perhaps the oldest biblical manuscripts known. Despite the war raging outside and the lack of proper film and lighting equipment—and even at times of electricity—Trever, a skilled photographer, succeeded in taking pictures of three of the scrolls, column by column. The fourth scroll proved impossible to unroll and was put aside.

Today, as the original scrolls have aged and faded, these photographs provide the only clear evidence of the existence of these lost words and letters. The photographer, Trever, sent prints to the most respected biblical archaeologist in America, Professor William Foxwell Albright of The Johns Hopkins

University in Baltimore. Albright quickly wrote back: "My heartiest congratulations on the greatest MS [manuscript] discovery of modern times!...What an absolutely incredible find. And there can happily not be the slightest doubt about the genuineness of the manuscript."

As May 15, 1948, the end of British rule in Palestine, approached, the fighting between Arabs and Jews increased. It seemed clear that the British were simply going to withdraw and let Arabs and Jews engage in a full-scale war. Meanwhile, the Americans received permission to publish photographs of the scrolls after convincing Mar Samuel that this would improve his chances of selling them for a good price. Then, in March, Mar Samuel sent, or took, the scrolls to Beirut. The Americans returned home. On April 11, 1948, a press release issued at Yale University in New Haven, where Millar Burrows was a professor, announced the recent discovery of the "earliest known manuscript" of Isaiah and three other ancient scrolls. Sukenik was outraged, certain that Kiraz had betrayed him. An entry in his diary says: "...the Jewish people have lost a precious heritage."

Within a few months of each other, two significant events occurred in Mar Samuel's life: He was declared an outlaw by the government of Jordan for illegally smuggling antiquities out of the country, and he was appointed apostolic delegate to the Syrian Orthodox Church in the United States and Canada.

During the battle for Jerusalem, St. Mark's had been shelled. Butros Sowmy was killed, and the monastery was severely damaged. Mar Samuel and his American partners maintained that he had performed a service by saving the scrolls from the bombardment and that the Jordanian authorities had been told about the scrolls but showed no interest. G. Lankester Harding, head of the Jordanian Department of Antiquities, argued that the scrolls had been shown to an assistant librarian at the Palestine Archaeological Museum, who had never reported this to his superiors. Mar Samuel moved to America in January 1949 and established a charitable trust to handle earnings from the scrolls. He hoped that selling the scrolls would raise enough money to repair the monastery in Jerusalem and also expand the church overseas. With the help of Trever and Burrows he exhibited his scrolls at the Library of Congress, the University of Chicago, Duke University, and other institutions.

In 1950 and 1951, Trever's photographs of the scrolls were published. However, contrary to the assurances he had received in Jerusalem, Mar Samuel now learned that experts were not eager to pay huge amounts for the original manuscripts when they had perfect copies to study. In addition, Sukenik and the government of Jordan made it clear that they considered the scrolls to be their property, and Anton Kiraz claimed that he had a deal with Mar Samuel giving him exclusive rights as seller of the scrolls. Yale University, which had so proudly announced the discovery of the scrolls and seemed eager to have them, lost interest. Buyers were now nowhere to be found.

Meanwhile, Lankester Harding had read about the scrolls in November 1948 and, as described in Chapter 1, found Cave 1 and excavated it in February 1949. He saw the number of broken jars and manuscript fragments at the site and realized that much more material was still in the hands of the Bedouin and outlaw dealers. As John Allegro, one of the original editors of the scrolls, says in *The Dead Sea Scrolls: A Reappraisal*, "a small piece of Dead Sea scroll may look very nice framed and hung over the mantel-piece, but it may well ruin the value of other larger pieces, depending for their sense on the inscription on the 'souvenir.'" Harding knew that if the fragmented scrolls were to be reconstructed and interpreted, all the fragments had to be collected. And this required quickly locating the still-unidentified dealer or dealers.

Once again, Harding turned to Joseph Sa'ad, secretary of the Palestine Archaeological Museum. Together, using a combination of threats and bribery, they tracked down Kando in Bethlehem. In February 1949 the war in Palestine was slowing down but not yet over, and Jordan had only recently taken over the proposed Palestinian state and international zone, which included Bethlehem. British-imposed law and order was gone, and Jordanian authority was not yet firmly established. Harding and Sa'ad knew that arresting Kando and his accomplices would be impossible. Instead, they chose to strike a deal with him.

Harding, a foreigner, stayed away from the dealings, while Sa'ad negotiated with Kando. Sa'ad convinced Kando that an English professor wanted to buy all the scroll fragments and guaranteed that no legal action would follow. With one of Harding's assistants posing as the professor, Sa'ad met Kando in Jericho to examine the fragments. It was well known by this time that Mar Samuel was in America asking a million dollars for his scrolls, and Kando expected the same kind of payment. A price of £1 ($4) per square centimeter was agreed upon, and as Sa'ad and Kando talked, the professor measured more than 1,200 sq. cm. of fragments. In the end, Kando accepted £1,000. This became the standard price for scroll material until a huge number of fragments flooded the market and drove the price down by half. But over the next few years, as other caves were discovered, the Bedouin received perhaps close to $100,000.

Meanwhile back in America, Mar Samuel had no luck finding a buyer for his scrolls. According to some reports, Yigael Yadin, recently retired as chief of staff of the Israel Defense Forces, offered to buy them but was refused. Finally, on June 1, 1954, Mar Samuel placed an ad in the *Wall Street Journal*: "THE FOUR DEAD SEA SCROLLS — Biblical Manuscripts dating back to at least 200 B.C. are for sale. This would be an ideal gift to an educational or religious institution by an individual or group. Box F 206, *Wall Street Journal*." Someone showed the ad to Yadin, now an archaeologist studying the scrolls bought by his father, Professor Sukenik, who had died in 1953. Drawing on his experience as a member of an underground army, the dashing Yadin arranged for a series of middlemen to buy the scrolls from Mar Samuel. Professor Harry Orlinsky, a Bible expert at Hebrew Union College, posed as a "Mr. Green" and met with a representative of Mar Samuel in the vault of a Chemical Bank branch in New York. After examining the scrolls, he telephoned a special number and said *"Le-chaim"*—Hebrew for "to life"—the code word meaning that the scrolls were authentic. Another middleman, Sidney Estridge, then paid $250,000 for the scrolls.

Six months later, on February 13, 1955, the prime minister of Israel publicly thanked Yadin for returning the four additional Dead Sea Scrolls to the people of Israel. Professor Albright had already been personally informed by Yadin and wrote to him, "How happy your father would be....These priceless documents belong at the Hebrew University." But when John Trever heard the news, he was bitter. Years later, in an interview included in Neil Asher Silberman's *The Hidden Scrolls*, Trever explained that at the time he was still committed to helping Mar Samuel find a buyer and admitted, "I was trying to find a way that would keep it out of the control of the Jews." Denying the anti-Semitism of his remark, he then added, "I felt that they really didn't have a right to do anything with these things." As for Mar Samuel, in 1991 he told the *Boston Globe*, "I never knew they would go to Israel. Now I'm sorry I sold them."

When we realize that in the United States during the 1950s, $6,000 was a desirable annual salary for a college graduate, and that in Israel a new car sold for about $700, it is clear that Israel, a newborn country flooded with war refugees, and Jordan, a poor land not yet rich in oil money, were paying immense sums of money to get the scrolls. Israel was assisted by a philanthropist, Samuel Gottesman, who repaid the loan that Yadin had taken to finance his purchase. Jordan, on the other hand, simply ran out of money. Harding persuaded his government to relax its antiquities laws by selling *ownership* of the manuscripts to foreign schools on condition that their *possession* remain in Jordan until study was completed. Beginning in 1954, Jordan sold the rights to various scrolls to, among other buyers, the Vatican, Oxford University, the University of Heidelberg, and McGill University in Montreal.

Although Kando kept insisting that all the scroll fragments had been handed over, every time more money came in, more fragments mysteriously appeared. The fragments were gathered into the Palestine Archaeological Museum in East Jerusalem, which had been taken over by Jordan. John D. Rockefeller agreed to pay the salaries of scroll experts, photographers, and support staff for six years. In 1960, when it was time to distribute the scrolls to the institutions that had bought them, the Jordanians suddenly hesitated. Muslim journalists and politicians, who until then had ignored these Jewish documents and the Christians studying them, protested the idea of westerners taking yet another collection of Middle Eastern treasures. In July 1960, the Jordanian government decided that scholarship and national pride would best be served if the scrolls were kept in Jordan. Despite protests, Jordan returned the money it had been paid for the manuscripts.

Meanwhile, the saga of Kando's scrolls continued. On August 1, 1960, Yigael Yadin was contacted by the Reverend Joe Uhrig and asked if he wanted to buy "important, authentic discoveries of Dead Sea Scrolls." Uhrig, host of the evangelical television show "Hand to Heaven," had visited the Holy Land in 1955. There he befriended his guide, Marcos Hazou, and the following year sponsored Hazou and his family as immigrants to the United States. Now, to repay the favor, Hazou informed Uhrig that his brother in Bethlehem had a friend named Kando who had scrolls for sale. Uhrig telephoned Professor Albright, who said that the scrolls belonged in Israel and suggested getting in touch with his friend Yadin. Uhrig and Yadin remember the details differently, but it seems that while the two men were exchanging letters over the next two months, Uhrig traveled to Bethlehem, something that Yadin, an Israeli Jew, could not do. There, Uhrig bought a fragment of the Psalm Scroll for $2,500. Back in America, he simply put the fragment into a manila envelope and then mailed it to Yadin. No sale price was mentioned. In October, Yadin sent Uhrig $7,000.

In May 1961, Uhrig offered Yadin an entire scroll. Again the two men remember the affair differently, but during their correspondence the price of the scroll seems to have gone up and down wildly, finally reaching a high of $750,000, as Kando kept changing his mind. At one point, Uhrig, negotiating in Bethlehem with Kando, tore off a dangling piece of the scroll and sent it to Yadin to prove his good faith. Eventually Yadin and Uhrig agreed on a sale price of $130,000 plus travel expenses. Yadin gave Uhrig $10,000 for the fragment, which he remembers as a down payment. Uhrig remembers it as an addition to the sale price.

In December 1961, Yadin received a letter from Uhrig asking for more money. Yadin asked for his money back. In May 1962, Uhrig wrote to say that the deal had fallen through but that he was keeping the $10,000 because Yadin had the fragment. In his account of the story, Yadin writes that he felt cheated—and perhaps conned. Uhrig, however, says that the problem was with Kando. He apparently expected to be paid in cash and was not satisfied with, or perhaps even acquainted with, bank drafts and contracts. Yadin gave up and went back to his excavations at Masada. Kando hid the scroll under his floor in a shoe box.

In November 1966, possibly because of anti-Western tension, Jordan took over the Palestine Archaeological Museum, which had been founded during the days of foreign rule, and dismissed its international trustees. The museum's treasures, which included the collection of Dead Sea Scrolls, became the property of the Jordanian government. In June 1967, war again broke out in the Middle East. In what came to be called the Six Day War, Israel soundly defeated Egypt, Jordan, and Syria and captured Jerusalem and Bethlehem. Even as the fighting continued, Yadin, who was military adviser to Israel's prime minister, seized the opportunity to send soldiers to Kando's house in Bethlehem where they found the scroll under the floor. They also discovered seventeen other manuscript fragments behind pictures, in a cigar box, and at Kando's brother's house. Although he confiscated the scroll on the spot, Yadin writes that he later paid Kando $105,000. Like Harding in Jordan, Yigael Yadin hoped that money rather than threats would bring additional manuscripts from their hiding places. "[I]t is a cloak-and-dagger business," he wrote in 1984. "I believe there still might be another scroll or some fragments out there."

After the war, Israel took over control of the Palestine Archaeological Museum and renamed it the Rockefeller Museum. *The Copper Scroll* and some other manuscripts had been moved to Amman, Jordan. But the truck that was supposed to transport the rest of the scrolls never arrived, and Israeli soldiers found them in the museum. Israel now had the Dead Sea Scrolls.

CHAPTER 3

The Mother of All Jigsaw Puzzles

Imagine if someone took 800 jigsaw puzzles, each containing 100 pieces, and dumped them into a large vat, mixed them around, and randomly discarded more than four-fifths of the 80,000 pieces. The remaining 15,000 to 20,000 pieces are bent, folded, spindled, twisted, and rolled out of shape. To add insult to injury, the edges are frayed and the design is faded beyond recognition. Now imagine being asked to assemble the original puzzles, without being told what they look like or how many there are. This, in essence, is what assembling the Dead Sea Scrolls was like.

Luckily, the first seven scrolls were relatively intact and recognizable, and for this reason the initial discovery of the scrolls caused worldwide excitement. The American Schools of Oriental Research could announce that it had an ancient copy of Isaiah, a commentary on Habakkuk, and a sectarian rule book. Eliezer Sukenik could say he had Isaiah, a collection of hymns, and an account of a war at the end of time. Even when these scrolls were damaged or incomplete, enough writing existed to allow a reader to understand the content, connect the broken pieces, and reconstruct the missing sections with some degree of confidence.

Even so, it took seven years for these manuscripts to be copied and published: the complete Isaiah and Habakkuk commentaries in 1950; the *Manual of Discipline* in 1951; the incomplete Isaiah, the *Thanksgiving Hymns,* and the *War Scroll* in 1954; and the *Genesis Apocryphon* in 1955. These publications offered photographs of the scrolls and translations of the text into modern Hebrew.

The fragments had a very different history. Some of them were large—a column or two, the top or bottom section of three or four columns, a few connected paragraphs. Some were small—a few lines or parts of a few lines. Some were as tiny as a single word or even part of a word. The fragments from Cave 1 were brought to the Palestine Archaeological Museum, where two men from the École Biblique, Fathers Jozef T. Milik and Dominique Barthélemy, sorted them. They were published in 1955 under the title *Qumran Cave 1,* Vol. 1 of the new series, *Discoveries in the Judaean Desert.*

With the discovery of Cave 4, however, nearly 15,000 fragments were brought in cigarette boxes and shoe boxes to the museum, where they were placed on rows of tables in the Scrollery, a long, narrow room with high windows. G. Lankester Harding, the Jordanian director of antiquities, asked Father Roland de Vaux of the École Biblique to recruit more experts who could move to Jerusalem for a year or so and work full-time at the museum. John D. Rockefeller agreed to pay their salaries for six years. Since the museum was an international institution, a mix of experts who balanced national and religious interests was desirable.

Recommendations were sought from trustees who were associated with the national schools of archaeology in

Jerusalem and from Bible experts in the represented countries. The resulting "International Team" included Fathers Roland de Vaux and Jean Starcky from France, Father Jozef Milik from Poland, John Strugnell and John Allegro from England, Frank Cross and Father Patrick Skehan from the United States, and Claus Hunzinger from Germany. The team also represented different religious viewpoints: four Catholics, three Protestants (one of whom later converted to Catholicism), and one non-religious person. Some of these men were established authorities; others were beginners, like John Strugnell and John Allegro, who were graduate students at Oxford University in Britain. Although some members of the team developed into important figures, it cannot be said that at the time of their appointment they were the best and the brightest experts available. In fact, some of the most qualified experts in the world simply were not invited.

Either by a clear order of the Jordanian government or by an unspoken "gentleman's agreement," no Jews were appointed. Even the Israelis, who took control of the scrolls in 1967, did not change this arrangement. Father de Vaux, who was anti-Israeli and at first refused to cooperate with the Israeli authorities, remained in his post. He was followed by Pierre Benoit in 1971 and in 1984 by John Strugnell, who publicly declared himself an "anti-Judaist." Whether this situation delayed or otherwise interfered with the interpretation of Jewish legal documents is still a matter of debate.

Unlike the scrolls from Cave 1, which were wrapped in linen and stored in sealed jars, the materials from Cave 4 seem to have fallen when the shelves on the walls deteriorated. They had spent hundreds of years stacked on the ground, exposed to weather, rodents, and insects. They were crumbling and disintegrating because they had been buried in layers of dirt on the cave floor. When the fragments arrived at the Scrollery, they were, in the words of Frank Cross, "warped, crinkled, or shrunken, crusted with soil chemicals, blackened by moisture and age."

The fragments were cleaned with a soft brush or a camel-hair brush dipped in castor oil. If they were too tightly curled to be flattened, they were placed on a shelf in a glass jar with water on the bottom. After a few minutes in the Middle Eastern heat, the moistened leather uncurled. But if it was not watched carefully, the leather would absorb too much moisture and rot, like the scroll in Kando's garden. After they were cleaned, the fragments were spread out between glass plates and displayed on rows of tables. At one time there were about 500 plates of unsorted material, each with dozens of fragments. Looking back, we can see how even the best intentions were not enough to prevent damage: The bright sun that streamed through the museum's high windows faded many of the fragments beyond recognition.

The experts took great time and care with the scrolls. A team member would take up a large fragment and then wander from table to table and from plate to plate looking for related pieces. Several factors worked in his favor. For one thing, very few of the manuscripts were written by the same person. Also, because many of the scrolls were the work of professional writers, or at least careful writers, they match in terms of width and length of columns and size and shape of letters. While they hardly match the magnificent artistic writing and illustrations of medieval manuscripts, the scrolls are examples of beautiful penmanship. Even the more careless or difficult handwriting has recognizable features.

The experts would look for pieces with matching characteristics: the nature of the material—whether parchment or papyrus—the color and texture, the language used, the number of lines in a column, the amount of space between lines, the width of a column, the size of the letters, the style of the script, the personal characteristics of the writer, the subject matter of the text. In this way all the pieces belonging to a particular manuscript were assembled in one place. The expert would then try to put together the text like a jigsaw puzzle—except that most of the pieces might be missing, or the edges might not be joined correctly, or the sequence of paragraphs or columns might be mere guesswork.

Sometimes, too, a worker would lose days or weeks interpreting what he thought was one text, only to discover that the same ancient scribe also had written two or three additional scrolls. In addition, he might find that a scroll had been written by two scribes or made by sewing together skins from different animals. The work in progress and the final glass-enclosed reconstruction were both photographed, usually by Najib Anton Albina, the Rockefeller Museum's photographer. Most of this type of sorting and compiling was completed by 1960, when the Rockefeller funding ended.

Cave 4 contained more than 500 manuscripts, which were assembled onto more than 600 plates. When the materials from all the caves had been accounted for, the team identified more than 800 different manuscripts—perhaps as many as 870—most written in Hebrew. About 20 percent were in Aramaic—a related Semitic language—and a few in Greek.

The next step was to reconstruct the texts and then analyze the meaning and importance of the message. This proved to be an overwhelming project, one that continues today.

Reconstructing a text involves filling in the missing sections with probable phrases and sentences. If the text is known, this is relatively easy. Almost any American can fill in the missing words in "I pledge...the flag of...States of America." This example is similar to what the team faced with biblical scrolls. When the text is unfamiliar, experts are aided by the skill of the original scribes, who created documents with consistent letter size and line spacing. A gap of a certain size must have contained a certain number of letters, and the scholar tries to find a meaningful word or phrase of the right length. If we measure a space two letters wide in "The child went...the store" we can assume that *to* is a more likely filler than *by* or *in*. If the space is four letters wide, we might consider *into* before *near*. Obviously, as the gap gets wider, the problem becomes more challenging. A huge gap in an incomplete text, as in "We...the...yesterday," is challenging. Unfortunately, many scroll fragments are frighteningly like this last example. Reconstructing such manuscripts requires almost as much creativity as composing them did.

A reconstructed text can always be challenged by alternative interpretations, using methods that were not available to the original team. In one such case, DNA (the material that codes genetic information in living things) in the leather has been analyzed to find out which pieces of leather belong to the same skin. In another, the patterns of decay have been analyzed. For example, because the scrolls were rolled up, an insect hole in a scroll will appear at the same height in each cycle, with each hole slightly closer to the next as the insect ate from the outer to the inner layers. By looking for similar holes in fragments, scholars have been able to align lines to the correct height and arrange columns in the proper order.

At first, the manuscripts were divided among the members of the International Team. The biblical texts went to Cross and Skehan, the Aramaic ones to Starcky, the commentaries and poetry to Allegro and Strugnell, and the sectarian documents to Milik. The team expected to publish their assignments within a few years. But without funding, the scroll project was no longer a full-time job. Teaching and other responsibilities slowed the pace of the team's work. Allegro published his twenty-nine texts quickly. Milik produced a great deal, but because of his brilliance, he had been given far more than even he could handle. Some of the editors would spend the rest of their careers—in one or two cases, the rest of their lives—working on the scrolls. Strugnell, who was twenty-four years old when he started, continued to publish parts of his texts even after he was removed from the team in 1990. If a member died or withdrew, his assignment was taken over by a new appointee. Hunzinger resigned and gave his material to Maurice Baillet. Eugene Ulrich inherited the assignment of Skehan, who died in 1980. But the size of the team did not increase. When it became obvious that eight men could not handle the huge task, some of the members gave scrolls to their graduate students. This practice caused resentment among other experts and eventually led to scandal and bitter fighting.

John Strugnell, who became chief editor in 1984, enlarged the team to twenty members (including several Jews) and issued a schedule for the publication of the remaining scrolls. However, excluded scholars—some of whom had waited thirty years to see material vital to their careers—remained unhappy. Many were stunned when Strugnell and Elisha Qimron presented a conference paper that year revealing some of the contents of *Miqṣat Maʿase ha-Torah,* also called the *Halakhic Letter.* Here was a document with specific details of the controversy between the Qumran sect and its opponents, a document that might help identify those opponents and the cause of their quarrel, a document that would change all histories of Second Temple Judaism—and it had been kept a secret.

Pressure to release the scrolls mounted. In September 1991, Ben-Zion Wacholder and Martin G. Abegg issued a computer-generated edition of some scrolls. During the late 1950s, the International Team had created an index listing the grammatical forms and locations of every word in the transcribed but unpublished scrolls. After becoming chief editor, Strugnell distributed this index to universities with scrolls scholars. By using computer software to cross-reference this information, the computer was able to reconstruct the original texts, which were published as *A Preliminary Edition of the Unpublished Dead Sea Scrolls* by Wacholder and Abegg.

Several weeks later, the Huntington Library in San Marino, California, offered qualified experts access to photographic negatives of the scrolls, which it had been given for safekeeping. Shortly thereafter, the final act began. Since 1989, an unnamed sympathizer had been sending scroll photographs to Robert Eisenman of California State University in Long Beach. Eisenman and James M. Robinson published these in *A Facsimile Edition of the Dead Sea Scrolls.* The books were hailed as a liberation of the scrolls and denounced as piracy. Critics said that the work of dedicated scholars had been stolen and published by others. Nonetheless, these newly available texts broke the complete hold over the scrolls that the International Team had. They opened a floodgate of new writings and ideas about the Dead Sea Scrolls.

As we have seen, reconstructing the scroll manuscripts required almost as much creativity as composing them did. In fact, this "creativity" was the issue of an important lawsuit. In 1994, John Strugnell and Elisha Qimron published *Qumran Cave 4-V: Miqṣat Maʿase ha-Torah* as the tenth volume in the series *Discoveries in the Judaean Desert*. *"Miqṣat Maʿase ha-Torah"* (MMT for short) means, approximately, "some details of the law" and contrasts the positions of the author and his opponents on certain aspects of Jewish law. Qimron and Strugnell had discussed this document at a conference in 1984 but would not allow other experts to look at it while they were editing it. A Polish journal of Qumran studies obtained a copy of Strugnell and Qimron's reconstruction and published it without their permission. In 1991, a copy of this unauthorized publication was included in *A Facsimile Edition of the Dead Sea Scrolls*, published by the Biblical Archaeology Society (BAS) in Washington, D.C. Qimron, who lives in Israel, sued BAS in an Israeli court for violating their rights to the work.

An author's creative work is protected by copyright. In other words, no one else can publish or benefit monetarily from the work without the author's permission until a certain number of years pass, when it becomes the property of the public, or "public domain." This applies to translations as well. Thus, while permission is required to quote from the Revised

English Bible of 1989, it is not necessary to quote from the King James Version of 1611 or to translate directly from the Hebrew or Greek bibles.

BAS argued in court that it had published a 2,000-year-old Hebrew text that was public domain. Qimron argued that because he had arranged seventy fragments from six different copies of MMT and reconstructed what the original looked like, he had created a work that belonged to him.

When invited to defend his suit in the pages of *Biblical Archaeology Review*, which is published by BAS, Qimron explained that reconstruction of the MMT was not like assembling a jigsaw puzzle. It was, he wrote, "a scientific undertaking that demanded an intimate knowledge of the relevant ancient literature; . . . above all it demanded creative imagination and authorship." More intriguing to future scholars, he also wrote that "we are far from claiming to have produced the only possible version of the text . . . if 100 thoroughly qualified editors were to edit the MMT fragments . . . the result would be exactly 100 different versions of the text."

The experience of other editors with other scrolls supports this astonishing statement. A fragment labeled 4Q448 (document 448 from Cave 4 at Qumran) has been reconstructed with the opening line, "A holy song for King Jonathan." This mention of a historical figure, Alexander Janneus (the only Jewish king named Jonathan) would provide vital evidence for dating the scrolls and for identifying the authors. But other experts reconstruct the same line as "holy city, joy of the king," which tells us nothing about the date or the author. Likewise, another fragment has been entitled "Ritual of Marriage." Such a document from Qumran would seriously strain the widely accepted belief that the people of Qumran did not marry or have children. But other experts read the text as part of a ritual honoring elderly members of the community. Recognizing the need for caution, scrolls scholars usually say that the fragments unearthed in the Qumran caves come from approximately 800 scrolls, representing about 500 different works. The content is equally divided among biblical, sectarian, and nonsectarian texts, with "sectarian" referring to the documents containing special rituals or beliefs of a separate Jewish sect, and "nonsectarian" meaning works of wider circulation, which may or may not have agreed with sectarian practice.

Dating the scrolls has proved to be as full of conflict as reconstructing them. When Mar Samuel brought his scrolls to the American Schools for assistance in dating them, John Trever, William Brownlee, and Millar Burrows searched the library for samples of ancient Hebrew scripts. But before the discovery of the scrolls, few ancient Hebrew documents existed. That is why the scrolls were such an unbelievable find. Until their discovery, the oldest surviving biblical manuscript in Hebrew was the Nash papyrus, a small fragment containing the Ten Commandments and Deuteronomy 6:4-5—the Shema´, so called because of its first word "Hear (O, Israel...)." The Nash papyrus was dated by Albright to the second century B.C. When Trever sent him photographs of Mar Samuel's *Isaiah Scroll*, he wrote back, "There is no doubt whatever in my mind that the script is more archaic [ancient] than that of the Nash Papyrus." Sukenik had already reached a similar conclusion, but not everyone was convinced. Solomon Zeitlin, in particular, used his position as editor of the *Jewish Quarterly Review* to argue that the scrolls were from medieval times.

As more scroll fragments were discovered, Albright and Sukenik's position became stronger. Finally, some of the documents could be dated to early Christian times. The letters from Bar-Kokhba and his commanders had to belong to the period of the Second Jewish Revolt against Rome (132-135 A.D.). And those found at Masada could only have been written before that rebel camp was captured by the Romans in 72 A.D. The scrolls from the Qumran caves were assumed to be even older than these because the Qumran settlement was destroyed in 68 A.D. Frank Moore Cross of the International Team took on the task of creating a relative time line based on paleography—the study of ancient written documents. For example, it is known that the shape of letters changes over time. If, for example, an angular letter becomes curved, as in the relationship between M/m, we would expect to see a gradual softening of corners as one evolved into the other, rather than a chance difference between forms. Therefore, if a number of manuscripts show variation in this letter, they can be sequenced in the most likely manner. If we are lucky, we might even find a general tendency, as in M/m, N/n, A/a, E/e, F/f. This is true, too, of letters that develop extensions above or below the line or that contain vertical and horizontal lines that cross. Since changes in several letters might occur at the same time, a correct sequence of manuscripts will, one hopes, account for all the changes. In this way Cross identified three periods in the Qumran scrolls: Archaic (250-150 B.C.), Hasmonean (150-30 B.C.), and Herodian (30 B.C.-70 A.D.). Only a few were Archaic. Most were Herodian.

For documents that are not dated internally, the sequence is harder to determine. To assign actual dates, other evidence is needed. For example, coins found in the excavations indicated when the sites were inhabited and also the latest date at which the manuscripts found there could have been written. The jars and broken pottery also were helpful since they could be compared with similar objects from locations with known dates. Later, the leather of the scrolls was tested by what scientists call the carbon 14 method, a method that dates ancient material by measuring the carbon contained in it.

More recently, the leather was dated using a sophisticated technique called accelerator mass spectrometry. Leather comes from animals, which absorb radioactivity from the environment. But the radioactivity starts breaking down as soon as the creature dies. By measuring the amount remaining, accelerator mass spectrometry can estimate when the animal died and thus when the leather—and the copies—might have been made. All of this evidence together builds the case for dating a scroll and placing it in relation to others. And this in turn highlights the damage done by the unsupervised fortune hunting of the Bedouin. Removed from the site of the find, scrolls purchased on the antiquities market often had lost much of their value for scholarship.

Additional evidence about the scrolls comes from the spelling and grammar found in them. Just as the English of Shakespeare and the King James Bible is easily recognized as differing from today's English, biblical Hebrew differs from Mishnaic, Medieval, and Modern Hebrew. Mishnaic Hebrew is the polished literary language of the great law code edited by Rabbi Judah Ha-Nasi ("the Prince") in the second century, not long after the Bar-Kokhba revolt. Again, because a language changes over time in a specific direction, the steps from one change to the next can logically be placed in sequence. The Hebrew of the Qumran scrolls is earlier than Mishnaic. In addition, even when a composition was written long before copies were made, as with the biblical texts, the Qumran scrolls show later spelling changes.

Archaeology and paleography, therefore, can guess with some certainty the dates when the scrolls were copied. But this is not the same as knowing when the originals were composed. Obviously, the biblical texts are much older than the Qumran copies—perhaps hundreds of years older. But what about the sectarian texts? Dating them has caused many disagreements. A great deal depends on what can be guessed at from their content and whether the scrolls are somehow related to the site where they were discovered. These questions are taken up in the following chapters.

CHAPTER 4

Voices Crying Out in the Wilderness

"Son of God." "Pierced Messiah." Phrases like these were sure to grab media attention when they turned up in the Dead Sea Scrolls. But were they sensational discoveries or merely sensationalism? One of the mysteries of the scrolls is determining what they really say. Yet, despite the best efforts of competent scholars, this is not always easy.

The first seven Dead Sea Scrolls included two copies of Isaiah, a commentary on Habakkuk, a version of Genesis, a collection of hymns, a manual for an ascetic—or hermit-like—sect, and a vision of the final war between good and evil. When the tens of thousands of additional fragments were assembled, it was clear that they came from more than 800 different scrolls. A few of these scrolls were nearly complete, and some were substantial portions. But others were represented by only a few lines or a few words. Most of the "scrolls" are fragments composed of many small pieces and tiny scraps. When assembled, the reconstructed columns contain large gaps. And, of course, much—or even most—of each work is missing entirely.

Without knowing the words and meanings of what surrounded them, many of the readable words and phrases are difficult to understand clearly, just as in English we cannot know whether the word *revolution* in isolation is the noun form of *revolve* or *revolt*, or whether "Pat's picture" is *of*, *by*, or *belonging to* Pat. To take just one example from the scrolls, the key Hebrew phrase *mwrh ṣdq* is generally translated as "Teacher of Righteousness," but it could also mean "righteous teacher" or "one who teaches correctly." Also, since the Hebrew alphabet does not use capital letters, differences like teacher/Teacher and law/Law in the English translations represent an editor's interpretation, not a definite and clear part of the original. In short, someone looking at several possible reconstructions of the same fragment would be startled by the differences. And someone reading several translations of a particular scroll fragment would find it hard to believe that the same text is involved.

Editors of the various scrolls generally give them titles that capture only what they think is significant, and other experts may disagree and assign different labels. Many texts now have widely accepted titles (frequently more than one), but most are known simply by a code that includes the location, cave, and a randomly given number (for example, 4Q499 = document 499 from Cave 4 at Qumran), or the location, cave, and a Hebrew abbreviation (for example, 1QH = *Hodayot "Thanksgiving Hymns"* from Qumran Cave 1). Those works that contain enough identifiable text can be divided into three categories of roughly equal size: Bible, sectarian, and other. Although the scroll of Isaiah received the place of honor in the first press release, the sectarian scrolls have provided enormous insights into the history of Second Temple Judaism and early Christianity. The following discussion is necessarily limited to a small fraction of the more than 200 sectarian scrolls. But it will give a sense of the sect's beliefs and practices, as well as the variety of its literary styles.

RULES

Some of the scrolls contain the rules of a reclusive sect of Jews generally believed to be the Essenes, some of whom lived at Qumran during the last two centuries of the Second Temple. These scrolls caused excitement among historians— and confusion among conservative Christians—because they pointed to similarities between the sect and the early church, making the sect's members seem like earlier versions of Christian monks, the holy men who lived very simple lives dedicated to faith and prayer.

Manual of Discipline

This was one of the seven original scrolls and was acquired by Mar Samuel. When Millar Burrows, director of the American Schools of Oriental Research in Jerusalem, examined the text, it reminded him of a Methodist "Manual of Discipline" and thereby received its title. It is also called "The Community Rule" and "The Rule of the Community." In addition to the copy in Cave 1, which contained eleven well-preserved columns, ten fragments were discovered in Cave 4 and two in Cave 5. Portions of this document also are quoted in other scrolls found near Qumran. Vermes dates the text to about 100 B.C. Gaster suggests that the *Manual of Discipline* may predate the Qumran sect, which then adopted its teachings as an ideal toward which to strive. Wise, Abegg, and Cook consider it the charter of a sectarian association called the *Yaḥad*, or "unity"—with many member chapters rather than just one particular community at Qumran. García Martínez believes that the many differences among the copies may be an indication of how the sect's (or sects') beliefs or situations changed over time.

An important passage in columns 3-4 of the *Manual of Discipline* gives the sect's view on predestination: All things are ordained by God and are part of his plan. In accordance with God's mysterious ways, humanity is divided into the Sons of Light and the Sons of Darkness. The former are ruled by the Prince of Light and are marked by charity, humility, goodness, wisdom, and a desire for justice. The latter are ruled by the Prince of Darkness and practice greed, pride, lust, impurity, and blasphemy (taking the name of God in vain). Although the spirits of darkness strive to destroy and torment the Sons of Light, God will not allow them to succeed, for he is their creator and superior. All people walk in both good and evil in different measures, depending on which spirit is greater within them. At the end of time, God will destroy evil and reward the upright.

The document reads like a guide for community leaders. It tells the leader to accept only those who have voluntarily given themselves over to God's law and who will obey the rules of the society, loving the Sons of Light and hating the Sons of Darkness. Then follows the ceremony that introduces new members into the community. In the presence of God, the priests and levites—assistants to the priests—pronounce a blessing and a curse over the new members, who reply "Amen, Amen." Expanding on Numbers 6:22-27, the priest says: "May he bless you with good and keep you from evil. May he enlighten your heart with insight and be gracious to you with knowledge...." The levites then pronounce a curse on anyone entering the community in falseness or hypocrisy. If, after a two-year trial period, the new member gains full acceptance, he gives his property to the society and may join in the communal meal.

Members must follow many rules. They must keep the laws of the Torah—the holy teachings of Judaism—as interpreted by the priests of the Zadokite family. The Zadokites were the "Sons of Zadok," or Righteous One. They must eat and worship together, always in the company of a priest. At public meetings each person speaks in order of rank when called. The supervisor is instructed not to bother correcting the behavior of outsiders. He should instead concentrate on correcting the chosen ones. Penance (a punishment for sins) is ordered for members who lie, abuse community property, or sleep during assemblies. The punishment for blasphemy is expulsion from the community.

Damascus Document

Also known as the *Damascus Covenant* and *Zadokite Fragment*, the text of this document has been available since 1910, when it was published by Solomon Schechter, a professor of rabbinic literature at Cambridge University. In 1896, Schechter received permission to remove documents from the *genizah*—an attic storage room—of the Ezra Synagogue in Old Cairo. Among the tens of thousands of dusty and deteriorating fragments were two partial copies, one from the tenth century and another from the twelfth, of the *Damascus Covenant*. The *Covenant* speaks of a religious sect that escaped persecution through its exile to Damascus, which may refer to the actual city in Syria or may be a code for some other location. Schechter believed that the sect in the document referred to the Karaites, a Jewish sect that accepts only the written Torah. When ten fragments of the original work were discovered at Qumran—eight in Cave 4 and one each in Caves 5 and 6—it was clear that the document came before the time when the Karaites broke off into a distinctive group. Vermes dates its composition to about 100 B.C., and one copy from Cave 4 has been dated to a period not long after that. 4Q265 seems to combine sections of this and the manual. The work falls into two parts: a history of the sect and a list of laws in the style of the Mishnah, which is a rabbinic work of the second century A.D.

The first section contains a history of a chosen group of Israelites, probably the group that wrote it. It is marked by quotations from Scripture that are interpreted in the sect's characteristic style. In the "age of wrath"—a time of trouble—390 years after the destruction of Jerusalem and the First Temple, God caused a root to blossom from the pious priests and children of Israel. For twenty years, they looked for the Way, until God raised up a Teacher of Righteousness (according to Gaster, "one who would teach the Law correctly") to impart the true meaning of his laws. There also arose a Scoffer or Liar who was joined by those who "remove borders," "seek smooth things," and "build walls." They misled the people through incorrect interpretations of the Law and brought down upon them all God's curses.

But just as in ages past those who kept the Law earned divine reward, so now, too, those who cling to God will gain eternal life. In support of this, the author quotes the prophet

Ezekiel (44:15): "The priests, levites and sons of Zadok who maintained my sanctuary when the children of Israel strayed shall offer me fat and blood." This is interpreted as follows: the priests are those who repent and leave the land of Judah, the levites are those who join them, and the sons of Zadok are those chosen by name who will remain at the end of time. Even in the time of evil, God will choose men to dig the well. As stated in Numbers 21:18, this is "a well which the princes dug, which the nobles of the people delved with staves." In other words, the well is the Law, those who dug it are the penitents—called princes—who left Judah for Damascus, and the staff is the interpreter of the Law. As in the *Manual of Discipline*, the chosen and condemned are known from the beginning. The wicked, for example, were rejected from the beginning of the world, and even before they were born, God knew their deeds (column 2, lines 7-8).

Those who join the community are warned against the traps of Belial: wealth, ritual impurity, and fornication. There follows a list of violations—e.g., blasphemy, desecration of the Temple, polygamy (marriage to more than one person at the same time), and forbidden marriages between an uncle and his niece—that by implication are practiced by the "builders of the wall."

In contrast, those who follow the proper path shall not enter the Temple for vain service, shall not swear oaths, shall not mingle with the Sons of the Pit, shall not seek wealth, shall not rob from the poor, and shall not fornicate. They shall distinguish the ritually pure from the impure, and the holy from the unholy; they shall keep the Sabbath, feasts, and fast days; they shall help the poor and the stranger; and they shall honor their vows to keep the commandments. Those who live in camps, marrying and begetting children, shall be careful to maintain the laws "between a man and his wife and between a father and his son" (Numbers 30:17). A large section lists rules of dress, bodily care, and restricted activities related to strict observance of the Sabbath, with the warning not to ask a non-Jew to perform work forbidden to a Jew. Other sections deal with the religious implications of skin disease, bodily discharges, marriage, and childbirth, and with such economic matters as business ethics.

An interesting rule (column IX), apparently interpreting Leviticus 27:29, is translated differently by the various editors of the *Damascus Covenant*. The verse in Leviticus reads: "No human who has been declared anathema can be ransomed; he must be put to death." For the rule explaining "anathemas" here, Gaster defines it this way: "... any man who, as the result of a private vow, gets a fellow human being doomed to death under the laws of the Gentiles is himself to be put to death." Vermes has: "Every vow by which a man vows another to destruction by the laws of the Gentiles shall himself be put to death." García Martínez reads: "Every man who gives a human person to anathema shall be executed according to the laws of the Gentiles." And in Wise, Abegg, and Cook the law is: "Any human being that any other human being is under a religious obligation to kill shall be put to death by the laws of the Gentiles."

4Q477

This fragmentary document, composed of about ten tiny pieces, seems to be an actual list of broken rules kept by the supervisor, in accordance with the guidelines in the *Manual of Discipline* and the *Damascus Document*. It is therefore important because it shows that these rules were actually followed by a real community. Esther Eshel believes that they were publicly announced by the *mebaqqer*, or "overseer." Because of the poor condition of the pieces and the large missing areas, reconstructions vary greatly. But there is agreement about some of the names of members and their violations. Johanan was short-tempered. Joseph had the evil eye. Hananiah Notos disturbed the community. Hananiah, son of Simon, committed sins of the flesh. Depending on the reconstruction of the word before flesh, he either indulged in the good life, had sexual relations with close relatives, or enjoyed bodily emissions.

LAWS

As more texts have become available and as Jews have been appointed to the editorial team, the focus of scroll study has expanded to include the changes in Jewish law and the development of rabbinic Judaism. The "builders of the wall" and "seekers after smooth things" have been identified with the Pharisees. In the section of the Mishnah known as *Avoth*, or "Fathers"—commonly called "Ethics of the Fathers"—the Men of Great Assembly teach, "Build a fence around the Law." By this they mean that permitted actions should be forbidden if they might lead to violations of biblical laws. For example, the Sabbath rest begins at sunset. By planning to end forbidden work a half hour before sunset, someone can miss the target time by a few minutes and still not violate the commandment. Similarly, Lawrence Schiffman argues in *Reclaiming the Dead Sea Scrolls* that the phrase *dorshe ḥalaqot*, usually translated as "seekers after smooth things," would be better translated as "interpreters of false laws." In his view, the Qumran sect opposed such expansion of the laws by the Pharisees, as well as interpretations that they considered improperly lenient. The Qumran sect accused the Pharisees of rejecting the clear words of the Torah and therefore declared them guilty of blasphemy (*Damascus Document*, column 5, line 13).

Temple Scroll

With sixty-six columns of text stretching more than twenty -seven feet, this is the longest of the Dead Sea Scrolls, longer than the *Isaiah Scroll* by five feet. Since the last column ends in the middle of a sentence, there originally was at least one additional column. The scroll may have been removed from Cave 11 in 1956. After negotiations with Kando failed, Yigael Yadin, Israel's most important biblical archaeologist at the time, obtained the scroll during the Six Day War of 1967. An additional fragment also was unearthed in Cave 11. Another fragment, 4Q365a, may be from this document or it could from what scrolls experts call a "reworked pentateuch," the original five books of the Old Testament. This uncertainty highlights once again the difficulty in interpreting the larger importance of the scrolls.

While the scroll is written in the style of Deuteronomy, from which it draws passages and laws, there is a significant difference: Deuteronomy is presented as the words of Moses conveying the message of God; in the scroll, God speaks in the first person. Also, the scroll fills in details missing from Deuteronomy and reconciles seemingly conflicting laws. Yadin gave it the title *Temple Scroll* because nearly half of the text is devoted to a detailed description of a magnificent Temple and its associated laws. Although the Torah specifies that there should be a centralized sanctuary in the Promised Land—"only at the place that God will choose...shall you bring your burnt-offerings and feast-offerings...your vow-offerings and your free-will offerings...." (Deuteronomy 12:4-19)—no instructions are given for building it. According to 1 Chronicles 28:11-19, King David gave his son Solomon a written plan for the Jerusalem Temple as revealed to him by God. Yadin believes that the author of the *Temple Scroll* may have considered himself divinely inspired to reconstruct or recover this lost document.

In like fashion, Deuteronomy 17:15-20 allows for the appointment of a king and warns him to observe the Torah and avoid acquiring excessive wealth. And when a monarchy finally was established by the prophet Samuel, he "explained to the people the laws of kingship and wrote them in a book which he placed before the Lord" (1 Samuel 10:25). But that book is lost, and another section of the scroll, which Yadin labels "Statutes of the King," fills in these missing laws. As for reconciling contradictions, the Bible forbids the eating of blood. Deuteronomy 12:23-24 says the blood must be poured on the ground like water; Leviticus 17:13 says it must be covered with earth. The scroll says: "...you shall pour it on the ground like water and cover it with earth."

The *Temple Scroll* includes holy days that are not mentioned in the Bible: the festivals of New Barley, New Wine, New Oil, and Wood Offering. In addition, many of the laws in the scroll are stricter than corresponding laws in the Torah or rabbinic Judaism. While column 66 repeats many of the prohibitions against incest from Leviticus 18, it also adds marriage between uncle and niece to the list, as the *Damascus Document* does. The scroll also extends the holiness of the Temple to the entire city of Jerusalem. Thus, sexual relations are forbidden in the city. Moreover, latrines—and their associated bodily functions—are banned from Jerusalem. In one of the great advances in public sanitation, Deuteronomy 23:10-15 says: "When you encamp against your enemies ... there shall be a place outside the camp where you may relieve yourself. A shovel shall be included among your gear, and when you go outside you shall dig with it and cover your excrement. For the Lord is in your camp." Since in the scroll Jerusalem also is considered the same as a camp, latrines had to be 3,000 cubits—about 4,500 feet—beyond the city gate, out of view.

Halakhic Letter

Halakhah is Jewish law, and this document was so named because editors John Strugnell and Elisha Qimron believe that it is a legal letter from the Teacher of Righteousness to the Wicked Priest. Hence the name *Halakhic Letter*. Based on a phrase that appears toward the end of the work, it is also known by the Hebrew title *Miqṣat Maʿase ha-Torah*, variously translated as "Some of the Works of the Torah," "Some Observances of the Law," or "Concerning Some Aspects of the Law." Cave 4 yielded six fragments of this work, totaling 120 lines. A sectarian calendar at the beginning of one of the scrolls may or may not belong to the *Halakhic Letter*.

As reconstructed, the *Halakhic Letter* lists twenty or so points of ritual law on which the writer ("we") and the addressee ("you") disagree, such as marriage, purity, the status of Jerusalem, and acceptance of sacrifices from Gentiles. The writer believes that priests should not "mix their seed," apparently meaning that they should marry only within priestly families. He also believes that the sanctity of the Temple extends to all of Jerusalem, and therefore dogs should not be allowed in the city. Some of the positions taken by the writer agree with opinions that the Talmud—a collection of rabbinic laws written several centuries later—credits to the Sadducees in their disputes with the Pharisees. In one such opinion, involving a stream of liquid being poured from a pure vessel to an impure one, the writer takes the strict view that the impurity runs upward against the flow and contaminates the pure vessel. These cases have led some scholars to argue either that the *Halakhic Letter* was authored by Sadducees or that the Qumran sect began among Sadducees unhappy with their sect. The nature of the disputes proves that the conflict between the Qumran sect and its enemies concerned observance of Jewish law, with both sides claiming to be the truly observant.

The letter ends with the writer explaining that he hopes his arguments will influence the addressee to correct his errors. The polite and friendly tone is in sharp contrast to the harsh, uncompromising lecturing in so much of the Qumran material: the *Manual of Discipline,* for example, which tells the instructor not to bother arguing with outsiders. This suggests to some scholars that the letter was written soon after the first conflict, when reconciliation still seemed possible and desirable.

COMMENTARIES

The Bible was central to the Dead Sea Scrolls sect. Well over 200 biblical scrolls were recovered from the Qumran caves, indicating the importance of Bible study. In addition, a large number of other scrolls are related to the Bible in various ways. Tobit is included in the Catholic Old Testament and the Protestant Apocrypha; Enoch is considered sacred by the Ethiopic Church, the Christian Church of Ethiopia. Copies of older stories like the *Genesis Apocryphon* were among the first seven scrolls discovered. Other manuscripts have editorial titles like *Reworked Pentateuch, Vision of Samuel,* and *Pseudo-Ezekiel.* Still others are sectarian commentaries on the Bible that assume that the biblical texts refer not to their own time but to the history of the sect. A characteristic style is the *pesher* (plural, *pesharim*), which derives its name from a Hebrew word meaning "interpret." In the typical formula, a biblical verse is followed by "interpreted this means" or "its interpretation is...." Sometimes a scroll comments on a book of the Bible verse by verse. Other times, verses from many books are collected in support of a particular theme. The *Florilegium,* for instance, shows that passages from Samuel and Psalms predict the two Messiahs, the Branch of David and the Interpreter of the Law.

Commentary on Habakkuk

This thirteen-column fragment was one of the first seven scrolls recovered and was published by scholars of the American Schools of Oriental Research. The commentary explains the biblical text as if the prophet is speaking about the history of the sect and therefore provides valuable information for the historian. Unfortunately, titles are used instead of names, so that there is considerable disagreement about exactly who is meant. The *pesher* tells how God has shown all the mysteries of the future to the Teacher of Righteousness, but traitors rejected the Teacher and joined the Man of Lies. They will not be saved among the loyal followers when the Kittim overrun the world with their horses and armies. Although the Wicked Priest was once loyal, when he gained power he betrayed God for the sake of money. However, in the final days, the wealth of the priests will fall to the Kittim. (Because the Kittim are said to offer sacrifices to their standards and to worship their weapons, they have been identified with the Romans, whose military practiced similar rituals.) This would support scientific evidence dating composition of the scroll to the Herodian era—the age of King Herod.

A much-discussed passage in column 11 (which we will look at again in the section on calendars later in this chapter) says that on the Day of Atonement the Wicked Priest pursued the Teacher of Righteousness to his place of exile with the intention of consuming or confusing him and making him stumble. A passage in column 9 says that because he tormented God's elect, the Wicked Priest was handed over to his enemies to be destroyed.

Commentary on Nahum

This brief fragment has captured public attention for a number of reasons. First, it uses actual names in addition to puzzling titles. One section speaks of a Greek king (only the end of the name, "trius," is legible) who was urged by the seekers of smooth things to enter Jerusalem, something that was not done from the time of Antiochus until the coming of the Kittim, or Romans. Antiochus may be the ruler Antiochus IV Epiphanes, whose harsh rule sparked the Maccabean revolt. Since the seekers after smooth things are the Pharisees, the Greek king may be Demetrius III Eucerus, who aided them in their fight against Alexander Janneus, who reigned from 103 to 76 B.C. Second, the commentary speaks of a Lion of Wrath or Angry Lion who "hangs men alive," that is, crucifies them—a practice that horrified the Jews. This, too, may refer to Alexander Janneus. According to the first-century Jewish historian Josephus, this king crucified 800 Pharisees who had supported Demetrius.

Before his official publication of this fragment appeared, John Allegro, a member of the original International Team, made the controversial announcement that the fragment mentioned the crucifixion of the Teacher of Righteousness, which drew a parallel to the story of Jesus. In a dramatic story complete with invented scenes, he told how the Lion of Wrath had dragged the Teacher from his Dead Sea home and executed him, and how the Qumran sect then recovered their Master's body "to stand guard over it until the Judgment Day." He later toned down this interpretation. In *The Dead Sea Scrolls: A Reappraisal*, he says only that the "reference to crucifixion in their writings...would find an explanation if some of their own number had been put to death in this way."

Commentary on Isaiah

The prophet Isaiah looms large in the Dead Sea Scrolls. In addition to the two scrolls in the original find, fragments of twenty other scrolls were unearthed, more than for any book of the Bible except Deuteronomy and Psalms. Fragments of six commentaries on Isaiah were also discovered in Caves 3 and 4. Although they are very poorly preserved, they show that certain passages were read as prophecies by the sect. Isaiah 11:1 ("A rod will come from the stem of Jesse") is interpreted as the Branch of David who will rise up at the end of days. And 11:3, which reads, "he shall not judge by what his eyes see," means that he will take instruction from the priests and follow their guidance.

ESCHATOLOGY

Eschatology is the study of last things, the end of time, the awesome "day of the Lord." In the last century or so of the Second Temple, especially when Judea suffered under the cruelty of the Roman occupiers, many Jews found comfort in the belief that a better day was coming. The promised "branch of David," the Messiah—from the Hebrew word *mashiah*, meaning "anointed one"—would lead the forces of good in a final victorious battle against the forces of evil, and God's kingdom would be established forever. This is a central theme in many of the Dead Sea Scrolls.

War Scroll

This badly preserved, nineteen-column manuscript was among the first seven Dead Sea Scrolls that surfaced in 1947. Professor Eliezer Sukenik, who acquired it for the Hebrew University, gave it the title "The War of the Sons of Light against the Sons of Darkness." Six related fragments were found in Cave 4, but it is unclear whether they represent different versions of this text, separate works on the same theme, or perhaps some of the source material. Yigael Yadin, who had served as chief of operations for the Israel Defense Forces before beginning his distinguished career in archaeology, believed that the military tactics described in the scroll resemble those of the Roman legion, not those of the earlier Greeks. This would identify the Kittim mentioned in the text as the Romans. Since the Kittim are said to rule the world and have a king, they are probably the citizens of Imperial Rome. The composition would then date to after 27 B.C., possibly during the reign of Herod the Great or even later. Because of its early discovery, this document played an important part in forming the portrait of the Qumran community. It might be considered the classic statement of their view of Armageddon: Despite terrible suffering and bloody setbacks, the Sons of Light will ultimately triumph by the hand of God, and a great age will dawn.

Further, the work predicts that the war will last forty years, with victory changing hands until God steps in. In sequence, the Sons of Light will subdue the nations of Shem, Ham, and Japhet, usually taken to mean Asia, Africa, and Europe. The order of battle is described in great detail—when the infantry should advance, when the slingers should throw and retire, when the spear-throwers should let fly and take cover, when the cavalry should charge. The great standard at the head of the army will read "The People of God." Another will say "The Fury of God is Kindled against Belial and His Company." And another will say, "Praises of God on the Ten-string Harp." The trumpets will be inscribed with slogans such as "The Army of God," "Summoned by God to the Council of Holiness," and "The Peace of God in the Camps of His Holy

Ones." Priests will accompany the army into battle; they will sound the trumpets for the advance, attack, pursuit, and return. But they will remain at a distance from the bloodshed so as not to be touched by ritual impurity from the corpses. Purity is also a must for the soldiers. They must abstain from sexual relations and must guard the sanitation of the camp by locating their latrines outside, as in the *Temple Scroll* and Deuteronomy 23. The scroll also contains speeches and prayers to encourage the soldiers before battle and a Thanksgiving ceremony to celebrate the victory. The plan of attack makes no provision for the confusion of battle or enemy counterplans. The plan will work and the enemy will comply because everything is ordained by God, who not only knows the future but makes it happen.

New Jerusalem

The good-luck greeting "Next Year in Jerusalem" has been a popular expression among Jews for more than 2,000 years. After the destruction of the First Temple in 586 B.C., the prophet Ezekiel (chapters 40-48) saw a vision of a rebuilt Jerusalem and a glorious Temple. Even after returning from the Babylonian Exile and rebuilding the Temple (though on a less impressive scale than Solomon's), Jews continued to hope or, as in the *Temple Scroll*, plan. In 4Q554-555 and 5Q15, an angel shows the narrator the Jerusalem of the future. It will extend roughly 18 by 13 miles, making it larger than any city of the ancient world. The angel measures the walls, gates, towers, stairs, streets, houses, and rooms. Experts believe that a few poorly preserved fragments from Caves 1, 2, and 11 also belong to this composition.

Rule of the Congregation

This short work is attached to the Cave 1 copy of the *Manual of Discipline* and received its title from the official editor, Dominique Barthélemy. Because of its content, however, Vermes calls it *The Messianic Rule* and dates it to the middle of the last century B.C. It lays out rules for the whole congregation of Israel "in the last days," under the supervision of the levites and the Zadokite priests. Each man will have a military or supporting function according to his strength and intelligence, but all jobs will be honored equally. The communal meal will be led by the Messiah of Israel and a priest, whom Vermes takes to be the Priest-Messiah, or Messiah of Aaron. Children too young for service will be educated in what García Martínez translates as the "book of HAGY" and Vermes translates as the "Book of Meditation." But a significant word is damaged: Some editors believe it says that the Messiah of Israel will be "revealed" by God, others that he will be "engendered"—or created—by God.

The Pierced Messiah

Robert Eisenman caused quite a stir in November 1991 when a press release announced his translation of 4Q285. This is a fragmentary manuscript composed of seven small pieces. Fragment 7 contains fewer than twenty words on six lines. In the reconstruction that Eisenman and Michael Wise include in *Dead Sea Scrolls Uncovered*, the first line refers to "Isaiah the prophet," the second seems to quote Isaiah 11:1, "A staff shall come from the stem of Jesse," and the third mentions "the branch of David." Eisenman and Wise propose that the fourth and fifth lines read: "...and they will put to death the Leader of the Community, the Branch of David .../... and with woundings...." Since "Branch of David" is a title of the Messiah, the obvious comparison to the crucifixion and piercing of Jesus gave the fragment its popular name—and caused an uproar in the press. However, this translation is not the only possible one. In Biblical Hebrew the verb typically stands before the subject and object of a sentence. The verb here is *hmytw*, in which the w could mark a plural subject ("they will put to death") or the object "him." Thus, as other experts have noted, and as Eisenman and Wise acknowledge in another reading, line 4 could be: "and the Leader of the Community, the Branch of David, will put him to death...."

WORSHIP

Many of the scrolls contain compositions that may have been important in personal prayer or communal worship. These include five copies of a meditation called *Barekhi nafshi*, from its opening words: "Bless, my soul, the Lord for all of his wonders." (In the Bible, Psalms 103 and 104 have a similar opening; Psalm 146 begins, "Praise, my soul, the Lord.") 4Q503, a manuscript reconstructed from more than 200 papyrus fragments, lists blessings for each day of the month. 1Q34 and 4Q507-9 offer prayers for festivals. Other manuscripts contain additional blessings and prayers for various occasions. García Martínez calls the poorly preserved 4Q414 a "Baptismal Liturgy," since ritual bathing was an important practice of the Qumran sect. Some scholars consider 4Q502 a marriage ceremony, but this is a very controversial interpretation.

Thanksgiving Hymns

One copy of this scroll was among those from Cave 1 that were acquired and published by Eliezer Sukenik of the Hebrew University. Fragments of six additional copies were unearthed in Cave 4 and one in Cave 3. Like some of the psalms in the Bible, these hymns refer to personal experiences of danger, persecution, and divine salvation. The author, who generally speaks in the first person, is convinced of his special chosen status and inspiration: "Brutal men seek my soul... they do not know that my office is from you." Many experts believe that these personal hymns were written by the Teacher of Righteousness. Vermes suggests that some may have been written by members to be recited at gatherings. He identifies Hymn 5 (22 in other editions) as appropriate for celebrating entry into the community: "I know that no riches equal Thy truth, and [have therefore desired to enter the Council of] Thy holiness."

The hymns reflect the two sides of chosen and rejected, of good and evil, of spirit and flesh. God decides from the beginning who is saved and who is condemned. The flesh is by nature low and sinful. In particular, sexuality is impure and disgusting.

Songs of the Sabbath Sacrifice

John Strugnell, a member of the original editorial team, published part of this work in 1960 under the title the *Angelic Liturgy.* The complete work was edited by his student Carol Newsome in 1985. Fragments of eight copies of this work come from Cave 4, one from Cave 11, and one from Masada. It contains songs to accompany the sacrifices offered on thirteen Sabbaths, that is, during one season, or one quarter, of the solar year; the introduction is "For the Master. Song of the sacrifice for the (number) Sabbath on the (number) day of the month." An important feature of these prayers is that they unite the earthly priests with the angelic choir singing them in heaven. Building on the "Throne of God" images in Ezekiel 1 and 10, the songs have the seven chariot thrones, and their animated wheels join in the worship. As with a lot of the sectarian literature from Qumran, the prayers also contain curses on those who reject the true path.

Psalms

The *Psalms Scroll*, which was discovered in Cave 11, includes a selection of biblical psalms, including a version of Psalm 151, which is found in the Greek Septuagint (a translation of the Old Testament from the third century B.C.) but not in the Hebrew Bible; two more that were known to the Syrian Christians as Psalms 154 and 155; and four others. Fragments containing additional psalm-like compositions also have been unearthed.

Column 27 of the Cave 11 scroll attributes to King David 3,600 psalms, including 364 songs to sing at the daily sacrifices; 52 songs for the Sabbath sacrifices; and 30 songs for the Day of Atonement, New Moon, and other festivals. While new moons are an aspect of the lunar (based on the cycles of the moon) calendar, 364 days and 52 weeks are from the solar (based on the earth's revolving around the sun) year. This is an important sectarian issue, as we will now see.

CALENDARS

The ancient Jewish calendar was based on the cycles of the moon. In fact, there are two Hebrew words for month: *yereh* derives from *yareah*, or "moon"; and *hodesh* comes from *hadash*, or "new (moon)." For ritual purposes each new month was declared by a religious court after the new moon had been observed. Depending on when this occurred, a month could have twenty-nine or thirty days. The standard lunar year consisted of 354 days. Because this was ten days shorter than the solar cycle that controlled the seasons, the lunar year fell progressively behind. To avoid such problems as having the "Spring Festival" of Passover fall in the winter, the court would periodically add an extra month—Second Adar—to the end of the year. This put the lunar and solar years back in the same time-frame with each other, and it also put Passover back in its proper season.

The Dead Sea Scrolls, however, are based on a solar year of 364 days. This is composed of fifty-two weeks, divided into four seasons of thirteen weeks each (7 x 13 = 91 days). Each season, in turn, is divided into three months of thirty days plus one "remembrance day" (3 x 30 = 90 + 1 = 91 days). Because all the key numbers are divisible by 7, holy days always fall on the same day of the week: New Year on Wednesday, Day of Atonement on Friday, Passover on Wednesday, Feast of Weeks (Pentecost) on Sunday. A practical outcome of following this calendar was that holy days for the Qumran sect were workdays for other Jews and vice versa. Because of this, the sect could not participate in Temple services, which, according to them, were always dated incorrectly. Likewise, they could never offer their own sacrifices at the Temple, controlled by priests using a different calendar. Several experts believe that this also explains why, as stated in the *Commentary on Habakkuk* (column 11, lines 6-8), the Wicked Priest came on the Day of Atonement to the "house of exile" of the Teacher of Righteousness to confront or attack him and to cause him to stumble. Vermes believes this is a deliberate challenge to the Teacher's calendar, since it was his holiest day but an ordinary day for the Wicked Priest. Wise, Abegg, and Cook say it was an attack that the Qumranites could not prevent without violating the Holy Day.

Calendars of various kinds are found among the Dead Sea Scrolls. In fact, one copy of the *Halakhic Letter* begins with a calendar. It may have been copied on the same parchment by coincidence. However, if it is an actual part of the work, then its inclusion would indicate the important role it played in the argument between the sectarians and the authorities in Jerusalem. Likewise, one fragment of the *Manual of Discipline* contains a calendar. A very fragmentary calendar includes historical references that Wise, Abegg, and Cook characterize as "maddeningly impossible to identify." Among the names they identify are Shelamzion (the Hebrew name of Salome Alexandra, the Hasmonean queen who reigned from 76 to 67 B.C.); Hyrcanus (her son, who ruled from 63 to 40 B.C.); and Aemilius (Marcus Aemilius Scaurus, a Roman general involved in the conquest of Jerusalem in 63 B.C.).

Mishmarot

The honor of leading the Temple service was divided among twenty-four priestly groupings, called in Hebrew *mishmarot*, or "watches." The Jewish priesthood (unlike the much later role of rabbi) was hereditary, beginning with Moses's brother Aaron. Two of Aaron's sons died childless (1 Chronicles 24:2); all priests therefore descended from the remaining sons, Eleazar and Ithamar. According to 1 Chronicles 24, David authorized Zadok of Eleazar's line and Ahimelech of Ithamar's to arrange the twenty-four priestly groupings, which are then named. This title, which brought status and income, was cherished over the centuries. While the Qumran sectarians rejected the existing Temple service and order, they expected to be thought of as the guardians of the true Temple in the messianic era—the time when the Messiah would come. They therefore carefully preserved their own record of the *mishmarot*. In a number of scrolls, calendars coordinate the priestly group, the lunar date, and the solar date; others name the priestly group that will serve at each holy day.

Enoch

The book of Enoch is not a Qumran document as such, but it is worth mentioning here because of its section on astronomy, or the study of the moon, sun, and stars. Fragments of eleven Aramaic copies emerged from Cave 4, one of which has been dated to about 200 B.C., before the Qumran sect was established. Before that, the text was known in an Ethiopic (an ancient language used among Christians in Ethiopia) translation, arranged into five separate, smaller parts. One of these, known as the Astronomical Book, contains information about the daily position of the sun and moon and the amount of light from the moon. For instance: "On the twenty-seventh of the month, it is six-sevenths covered. Then it rises and shines the rest of the night with a seventh and grows the next day to six and a half sevenths." Almost all of these details were left out of the Ethiopic translation; they were recovered only from the Qumran scrolls, which gives some idea of their value to the sect.

Jubilees

This is another book that was known before the Dead Sea Scrolls were discovered; it was probably valued by the sect because of its calendar. Fifteen (possibly sixteen) copies were found in Caves 1, 2, 3, 4, and 11, showing its importance at Qumran. In Leviticus 25, Moses is told to begin an agricultural and economic cycle of seven years: "Six years you may work your fields...but in the seventh the land shall have a sabbath rest." After seven cycles of seven years, there is a special "Jubilee," with the commandment to "proclaim liberty throughout all the land unto all the inhabitants thereof" (25:10—a verse inscribed on the Liberty Bell). Rented property is returned; slaves and servants are released. The book of Jubilees reviews Jewish history in units of forty-nine years (7 x 7). It also includes a defense of the 364-day solar calendar.

Horoscopes

Two fragments have been labeled horoscopes because they associate birth dates with certain physical traits. 4Q561 is a tiny scrap in Aramaic. 4Q186, in Hebrew, states that someone born in the foot of Taurus will have long and lean thighs and thin toes. His spirit is six parts light and three parts darkness. This strange text is written from left to right (instead of the usual Hebrew right-to-left direction) in a code composed of "square" Hebrew letters, ancient Hebrew, and Greek script. The reason for this, however, remains a mystery.

CHAPTER 5

The Treasure Map

One of the lasting mysteries of the Dead Sea Scrolls is the *Copper Scroll*. Discovered in March 1952 in Cave 3, which also contained remains of manuscripts, jars, lids, and a lamp, it is different from the other scrolls in material, language, and content. A great deal of our understanding of the Qumran sect depends on whether the *Copper Scroll* was produced by the same people who wrote the other scrolls or found its way to a scroll cave only by accident.

All the other Qumran scrolls are leather or papyrus, the normal writing materials of ancient Judea. The *Copper Scroll*, as its name indicates, is metal—sheets of thin copper connected by rivets. When the two pieces of the scroll were first found, one on top of the other, they were mistaken for two separate scrolls. But later examination showed that one set of rivets had given way as the scroll was being rolled up. When intact, the complete scroll was about 8 feet long by 11 inches high. Since exposure to the elements had weakened the copper, attempts to unroll the two scrolls caused the brittle edges to crumble and fall off. The scrolls were coated in wax when they were transported to the Palestine Archaeological Museum. All that could be seen were backward letters on the outside layer, a reverse image of the message that had been pressed onto the face of the copper sheets, which were then rolled inward. K. G. Kuhn, a professor from Göttingen, Germany, who was visiting Jerusalem, read enough of the visible writing to identify the scroll as a list of treasures. He guessed that the treasure belonged to the settlement at Qumran.

In the early 1950s, some chemists at The Johns Hopkins University in Baltimore were experimenting with ways to reverse the rusting of metal. The chemical composition of the two copper scrolls was studied, and the scrolls team hoped that a technique would be found for returning enough flexibility to the scrolls to allow them to be unrolled. But this did not happen. For three years, the two scrolls remained unopened and unread. Even after scholars decided to cut the scrolls open, each attempt threatened to break the fragile metal into tiny bits of dust. Then in 1955, John Allegro, who was associated with the University of Manchester in England, suggested that one of the scrolls be sent to the Manchester College of Science and Technology. There, Professor H. Wright Baker came up with a method for cutting it open. The rolled-up scroll was first coated with adhesive and heated to between 40 and 50 degrees Celsius. Then it was placed on a movable trolley and passed lengthwise under a tiny, high-speed circular saw. In this way a vertical slice of the first layer was removed. Dust and shavings were vacuumed and brushed away, and the scroll was rotated. Then another vertical slice was cut. In all, twenty-three vertical sections were produced. Still too brittle to flatten, they were placed side by side so that the writing could be read.

Allegro reported this success to G. Lankester Harding in Jerusalem, and the second scroll was sent to Manchester. When this was opened and read, the two scrolls were recognized as the parts of a single scroll containing twelve columns.

After the scroll was studied, it was placed in specially built display cases of wood lined with velvet in the Archaeological Museum in Amman, Jordan. Therefore, it was not in the Rockefeller Museum when the Israelis captured Jordanian-controlled East Jerusalem in 1967.

Although the scroll had been assigned to Jozef Milik for editing, Allegro, a brash and enthusiastic young man with a flair for drama, transcribed and translated it. The scroll contained a list of treasures—gold, silver, sacred vessels, oils, spices, and books—said to be buried in sixty-four locations. The directions are precise: "In the cistern below the rampart, on the east side, in a hollowed out rock: six bars of silver." "In the plastered cistern, down toward the left, three cubits from the bottom: forty talents [coins] of silver." "In the pool east of Kokhlit, at the north, dig down four cubits: twenty-two talents." Many of the sites cannot be identified—for instance, the garden of Zadok, the ford, or stream, of the High Priest—but most seem to be in a triangle bounded by Jerusalem to the west, Jericho to the east, and Qumran to the south. Some are beyond this triangle. For instance, Mount Gerizim, the holy place of the Samaritans, is thirty miles north of Jerusalem (unless a different place with this name is meant).

Apparently Allegro became so excited about this find, he could not wait for Milik to prepare the official publication. He published his own transcription and translation in *The Treasure of the Copper Scroll* in 1960, two years before Milik's study appeared in Volume 3 of the official series, *Discoveries in the Judean Desert*. Allegro insisted that the director of the Jordanian Department of Antiquities had authorized him to publish his book.

But Father Roland de Vaux, head of the International Team, insisted that only the official editors could assign scrolls for publication. Their anger over what they considered a violation of the gentlemanly rules of scholarship separated Allegro from the rest of the International Team. In the acknowledgments section of his own book, Milik actually goes out of his way to say, "I do not, however, take notice of the book by J. M. Allegro." The two books give very different transcriptions and translations of the text of the scroll, leading Theodor H. Gaster to decline in the 1964 edition of his book, *The Dead Sea Scriptures*, to include his own translation until photographs were published and he could see the text for himself.

Even before the scroll was published, Father de Vaux had announced his opinion that the treasure was imaginary. Allegro, however, was convinced that the treasure was real. Copper was an expensive metal. Punching 3,000 letters—ten strokes to the letter—into the metal was a difficult and time-consuming task. The actual writing on the *Copper Scroll* was a businesslike list of bookkeeping entries, without any accompanying stories or explanation. Allegro could not imagine anyone spending that kind of money and effort on fiction. He raised funds in England for a treasure hunt and received permission from the Jordanian government, which controlled the territory described in the scroll, to explore the area. Previous excavations led by Roland de Vaux at Qumran had uncovered three earthen jugs containing a hoard of 500 silver coins buried under the floor in one of the rooms. Allegro was sure that Secacah, a place mentioned several times in the scroll, was Qumran, and he dug there. He also sought permission from the custodian of the Mosque of Omar, the Dome of the Rock in Jerusalem, to tunnel under the terrace, but Jordanian soldiers stopped him.

The expedition for buried treasure was an embarrassing failure, producing only a few coins and pottery. Allegro must have seemed like a crazy person threatening to sink the International Team's scholarship. De Vaux wrote an article in 1961 describing Allegro's explorations as having "no serious archaeological authority" and charging that they had "eviscerated [destroyed] the soil and the walls of Khirbet Qumran." Allegro answered that since the official team did not believe that the treasure was real, they were not going to try to find it.

In his edition of the scroll, Milik declared the treasure a fiction that had been given a false air of truth by the precision of the geographical details. According to his calculations, the treasures listed in the scroll contained 4,630 talents of gold and silver. Depending on various estimates of what a talent weighed in those days, this came to between 58 and 174 tons of precious metal. Because in his view the Qumran sectarians were monks who had taken vows of poverty and lived by the sweat of their brows in the desert, Milik insisted that they could not possibly have had so much wealth. The scroll, he concluded, was just another of those Eastern tales of fantastic treasure, similar to the unbelievable Jewish legends about the wealth of King Solomon.

While he does not dismiss the possibility of innocent fiction, Theodor Gaster believes that the *Copper Scroll* "was intended to be taken seriously." He suggests that fraud or a cruel joke may have been involved. He notes that according to the first-century Jewish historian Josephus, the Samaritans had been the victims of such a hoax. When Pontius Pilate was the emperor's agent in Judea (26-36 A.D.), a Samaritan pretender tried to gain support by promising the people that he would show them where Moses had hidden sacred vessels on Mount Gerizim, the site of their temple before its destruction in 128 B.C. After Roman soldiers attacked the crowd going to the mountain, the Samaritans protested and Pilate was recalled to Rome. Gaster calls attention also to a Jewish legend that certain levites (assistants to priests) had an inscribed copper tablet listing the hiding places of the treasures of Solomon's Temple, destroyed by the Babylonians hundreds of years earlier. He guesses that a Jewish pretender may have taken advantage of a similar belief, attempting to reinforce his position by exhibiting such a document.

Other experts accept Allegro's reasoning that the time and effort invested in creating the expensive scroll suggest that the treasure is real. Edmund Wilson writes in "The Dead Sea Scrolls, 1947-1969," in *Israel and the Dead Sea Scrolls*: "I agree with Allegro that this list is too...businesslike not to indicate genuine treasures." And Geza Vermes says in *The Complete Dead Sea Scrolls in English*, "From the business-like approach, and the enduring material on which the catalogue is inscribed, it might sensibly be supposed that the writer was not indulging some frivolous dream." In addition, Milik's dismissal of the treasure is tied to his belief that the *Copper Scroll* belonged to the Qumran sect, whose members had taken vows of poverty. But Vermes accepts the viewpoint that, while the individuals may have kept nothing, the community may have profited from the wealth of its members.

Others, however, question the connection between the scroll and Qumran. The difference in the script between this and the other scrolls could be explained by the difficulty of inscribing letters on metal. But this does not explain why a work of fiction would be saved on expensive copper. It also does not explain why the particular form of Hebrew used in the scroll differs from the language of the other Qumran scrolls. On the other hand, if another group—from a different time or place—was responsible, the difference in language is understandable. And if the treasure was real, it made sense to preserve the locations on something more lasting than parchment or papyrus. A likely source of the treasure, these experts say, was the Temple in Jerusalem, because in addition to gold and silver, the hiding places mentioned in the scroll also contained sacred vessels, incense, and vestments, or holy items of clothing. And the likely author of the scroll was a priest of the Temple who, along with his fellow priests, hoped to hide the sacred treasure from the approaching Roman legions during the First Jewish Revolt of 68-73 A.D. Or perhaps the treasure was stolen and later hidden by the Zealots, who organized the defense of Jerusalem. In either case, the *Copper Scroll* describes hiding places of real Temple treasure and should therefore be dated to within a few years of 70 A.D., when the Romans destroyed the Temple.

This is the view of C. Kyle McCarter, professor of Biblical and Near Eastern Studies at The Johns Hopkins University and editor of a new edition of the *Copper Scroll* for Princeton University Press. If the treasure is imaginary, "it was imagined by someone who did not have too much imagination," he says. Further, he believes that the *Copper Scroll* has no connection to the Qumran sect. In support of the "extraordinary coincidence" that it was independently placed in a cave holding the

Qumran material, he notes that the scroll was not found in the same location as the manuscript fragments and broken pottery but was alone in the rear of the cave. Even de Vaux had noted this and had entertained the possibility that the two sites in the cave were not related. (This, by the way, again shows how important it was to have complete details of the place where the scrolls were found.)

McCarter argues that one of the hiding places mentioned in the *Copper Scroll* is an especially important piece of evidence linking the treasure to the Jerusalem Temple. According to his translation, column 7, line 8 locates six bars of gold "in the cave that is next to the fountain belonging to the house of Hakkoz." McCarter points out that Hakkoz is the name of a priestly family mentioned several times in the Bible. In the list (in Nehemiah 3) of those who helped rebuild Jerusalem after the Babylonian Exile, the Hakkoz family is included among the residents of the Jericho vicinity. This area, it will be remembered, is within the triangle outlined in the scroll. Moreover, Nehemiah 3:4 names a Meremoth, son of Uriah, as a member of the Hakkoz family, and Ezra 8:33 says that a Meremoth, son of Uriah—whom McCarter identifies as the same person—guarded the silver, gold, and vessels of the Temple. This would certainly explain why part of the treasure was buried on his property.

To appreciate why McCarter is publishing another edition of the scroll with new, high-resolution photographs, a word about the previous photos is necessary. The photographs taken in the 1950s and published in Milik's edition are so grainy and fuzzy that experts depend instead on his or Allegro's written copies of the Hebrew letters. But this raises another difficulty, which we can understand by comparing McCarter's translation of the line, "In the cave that is next to the fountain belonging to the House of Hakkoz," with those of Vermes and García Martínez. Vermes locates the silver "in the nearby cave in the [area] of Bet ha-Qos." García Martínez's translation reads: "In the cavity next to it, in the vicinity of Beth-Chagosh." The translations of Vermes and García Martínez do not have a fountain; the cave is next to or near the hiding place in the previous line.

Even more striking, there is no House of Hakkoz. While Bet/Beth means "house," both translations take this word as part of a name, like Beth-lehem or Beth-el. As for Hakkoz, Vermes takes *ha-* to be the article "the"; *Qos* is therefore a noun used as a name, like *Bet(h)*. García Martínez, on the other hand, seems to have read the Hebrew letters differently. The *ch* of *Chagosh* suggests that he sees the Hebrew letter *ḥet* where McCarter and Vermes see *he*, a reasonable disagreement respecting the Qumran script. But his *g* and *sh* in contrast to their *q/k* and *z/s* are harder to explain, since he normally transliterates *qoph* and *ṣade* as they do. Contrasts like these exist on almost every line in the various translations, especially with names. Just as in English speech there are differences in meaning in "The cooks/Cooks agreed with the bakers/Bakers," in the *Copper Scroll*, "Horebah" can be a name or "the ruin," and "in the Vale of Achor under the steps" can be "in the valley, go behind, under the steps," and so on.

Words that are no longer in use pose yet another problem in the *Copper Scroll*. In arguing that the treasure belonged to the Temple and not to the Qumran community, McCarter credits the contribution of Manfred Lehmann in decoding the technical vocabulary of the *Copper Scroll.* In a 1964 article in *Revue de Qumran*, Lehmann argued that, while the treasure did belong to the Temple, it did not reach Jerusalem because it was collected after the Temple had been destroyed. Interestingly, Lehmann begins with the idea that Allegro, Milik, and the other Christian scroll scholars had mistranslated key words in the *Copper Scroll* because they were unfamiliar with the legal terms used in the Jewish Temple. (Imagine, for example, someone who speaks English but who does not know baseball reading this sentence: "In the bottom of the fifth with two on and two out and the cleanup batter on deck, the pitcher stepped off the mound to check his signs.") For example, Milik translates *kli dema'* as "aromatic vases." But *dema'* is the technical term for a certain type of agricultural tithe, or payment; the vessels were therefore probably some sort of measuring bowl for the tithe.

So, too, the technical terms *ma'aser sheni* ("second tithe") and *ḥerem* ("consecrated offering") are incorrectly translated by Milik as "a second [offering]" and "condemned matter." Thus by drawing extensively on talmudic and rabbinic sources that were unknown to the members of the International Team, Lehmann showed that Temple taxes and tithes were collected for many years after the Temple's destruction in 70 A.D. Just as Solomon's Temple had been destroyed by the Babylonians 500 years earlier and a new Temple had replaced it, so, too, many Jews believed, this destroyed Temple also would be rebuilt. In the meantime, they continued voluntarily to pay their taxes and tithes. But because these funds were sacred and could not be used, the rabbis recommended that they be buried or, according to one ruling (Bekhoroth 53a), "thrown into the Dead Sea." The hiding places listed in the *Copper Scroll*, said Lehmann, contained this buried treasure, which the Romans eventually found and seized.

Even if there is no buried treasure, there is a wealth of information about language and geography in the *Copper Scroll*. The Hebrew language of the *Copper Scroll* is different from that in other Qumran scrolls. This may be due to errors in spelling and grammar, or possibly the scroll reflects a different time and place. Perhaps the writer was not a professional scribe and wrote in his local or spoken version of Hebrew. Obviously, records that reflect true speech are rare among the written records of any language, and if this is one such example it is extremely valuable. In addition, many Hebrew place names that were formerly known only in corrupted Greek form can now be seen in the original. For example, Jerusalem is divided by the Tyropoeon Valley, a Greek name that means "cheese-makers." However, as John Allegro explains in *The Dead Sea Scrolls: A Reappraisal*, the *Copper Scroll* refers to a *ge ḥiṣona*, or "outer valley." Since there is a root *ḥwṣ* meaning "curdle," which could have given rise to *ḥiṣona*, or "cheese making," two similar words were confused in translation: Outer Valley became Cheesemakers Valley. Similarly, the famous healing pool of Bethesda mentioned in Greek form in John 5:2 ("There is in Jerusalem...a pool which is called Bethesda in Hebrew....") has long confused experts. Some believe it got its name from "House of Esda," or *beth ḥesed*, "house of mercy." In some Greek manuscripts of John it appears as "Bethzatha" or "Bethsaida." The *Copper Scroll* shows, however, that the name is *Beth ʿEshda*, "the place of pouring," and that it also occurred in the dual form *ʿeshdatain*, "two pourings."

The final word on the *Copper Scroll* and its treasure has yet to be written; much of it is still a mystery. For example, experts suspect that both the fantastic amounts of gold and silver and their hiding places are parts of a clever code. Why, for instance, is this Hebrew document full of secret symbols in Greek letters, which nobody has yet been able to interpret? In addition, the last location listed—north of Kokhlit, near the tombs—is said to contain another copy of this list "with explanations, measurements and details of every item." Perhaps the *Copper Scroll* will reveal its secrets when this second clue is found, or when someone programs a computer to break the code. Until then, the mystery remains.

CHAPTER 6

Sadducees, Pharisees, Essenes, and Others

When Yale University announced in April 1948 that the oldest manuscript of Isaiah had been discovered, the press release also spoke of a scroll that "seemed to be a manual of discipline of some comparatively little-known sect or monastic order, possibly the Essenes." But at the time very little was known about Jewish sects in general and even less about sects in the second and first centuries B.C., when many of the Dead Sea Scrolls were written. Experts had heard of Jewish sects such as the Pharisees, Sadducees, and Essenes, but the differences among them were not very well understood.

Anyone who carefully reads the Hebrew Bible recognizes that there are differences in tone and outlook among the various books. The contrast between the Song of Songs and Lamentations can be explained by their differing subjects. But the differing worldviews in Deuteronomy and Ecclesiastes are harder to explain. Some prophets and storytellers in the Bible accept God's power with joy, while others seem to fear that power. Although many people believe that the Bible contains a single, united message, it is actually many books written by many people over hundreds of years bound into a single volume, the Bible. Perhaps Jewish thought—even inspired thought—changed and grew during these centuries. Certainly, the enormous amount of literature that was *not* put into the Bible was very different in religious and philosophical belief. Between the end of the Hebrew Bible and the beginning of Christianity—the "inter-testamental" period between the Old and New Testaments—many Jewish works were produced. A few were bound with the third-century-B.C. Greek Bible translation known as the Septuagint and became part of the Catholic Old Testament and Protestant Apocrypha. Others were considered less sacred but were studied nonetheless and have survived in non-biblical collections. Most, apparently, simply disappeared.

The texts that survive illustrate the many different kinds of Jewish thought in the centuries immediately before the rise of Christianity. Many of the ideas that are taken for granted in the New Testament are hardly mentioned in the Old Testament. Such concepts, including those of angels and demons and of reward and punishment in the afterlife, are well-represented in the post-biblical Jewish writings. One possible source of these new ideas is the changed world of Judea. Throughout most of the Hebrew Bible, the Holy Land—the kingdoms of Judah and Israel—is part of a Near Eastern culture that includes, or is dominated by, Egypt, Assyria, or Babylonia. When the Hebrew Bible ends, Judea is under Persian rule. Persia gives way to Greece. And when the New Testament begins, the Romans are in control. The inter-testamental literature demonstrates the new influence of Greek ideas on Jewish religious thinking. In particular, a whole school of "wisdom literature" developed, some of it previously known, such as the Wisdom of Ben Sira and the Wisdom of

Solomon, but much of it came from the Qumran caves. In this school of thought, the Torah, for example, becomes identified with the Greek Wisdom. This divine force is older than creation and may be what the Gospel of John understands by "In the beginning was the Word."

The Wisdom of Ben Sira, also called the Wisdom of Jesus (Greek for Joshua) Son of Sira, was highly regarded and frequently quoted by rabbinic and early Christian authors. The book was previously known in the Greek version of the Apocrypha; a small Hebrew fragment was discovered in Qumran Cave 2 and a larger Hebrew fragment at Masada. The author, a Palestinian Jew, was probably living at the same time as the high priest Simon, son of Onias, who died in 196 B.C. Most of the book is advice about public morality and private behavior. Although the author claims only extensive research, not divine inspiration—"I rose up last of all, as one that gathers after the grape gatherers" (33:16)—he praises religion as the basis of a meaningful life: "All wisdom comes from the Lord" (1:1), and "To fear the Lord is the beginning of wisdom" (1:14). On the other hand, "The beginning of pride is when one departs from God.... For pride is the beginning of sin" (10:12-13). He counsels readers to honor their parents, to be honest in business, to deal fairly with the poor and the weak, and to show compassion to the afflicted. However, Ben Sira clearly rejects the notion of an afterlife: "Thanksgiving perishes from the dead, as from one that is not:... man is not immortal" (17:28-30).

In contrast, the Wisdom of Solomon, a major philosophical work in which a traditional Jew adapts Greek thought, accepts the immortality of the soul: "God created man to be immortal, and made him to be an image of his own immortality" (2:23). The soul receives reward and punishment in the afterlife: "The souls of the righteous are in the hand of God, and there shall no torment touch them. In the sight of the unwise they seemed to die...but they are in peace" (3:1-3). Denial of the soul's immortality leads to sin: "For the ungodly said.... Our life is short and tedious...our spirit shall vanish as the soft air.... Come on therefore, let us enjoy the good things that are present" (2:1-6). Such thoughts lead to blasphemy and evil: "If the just man be the son of God, he will help him, and deliver him from the hand of his enemies. Let us examine him with despitefulness and torture" (2:17-19). Specific Greek influences are seen in a hymn to Wisdom, "a pure influence flowing from the glory of the Almighty" (7:25).

While Ben Sira and the Wisdom of Solomon disagree about basic issues, they are not identified with particular parties or sects. However, as 1 and 2 Maccabees show, by the beginning of the second century B.C., Jews were bitterly divided over how to deal with Greek influence. Some felt that Greek ideas were the wave of the future, the key to participating in the larger world. Others felt that it was a pagan threat to their ancestral faith and national identity. Still others looked for ways to adapt the new ideas to their religion or to accommodate their religion to the new world.

Greek influences had already reached the eastern Mediterranean by the end of the second millennium B.C., as can be seen in new ideas in architecture, ship design, military equipment, and perhaps iron technology. This contact continued even when Judea was a Persian territory. But how to deal with Greek influence became a matter of national survival when Alexander the Great conquered Judea in 332 B.C. After his death, his empire was divided among his generals, with Judea coming under the rule sometimes of the Ptolemies of Egypt and sometimes of the Seleucids—a dynasty from Syria. In 198 B.C. the land of Israel fell to Antiochus III of Syria. In 175 B.C., during the reign of Antiochus IV Epiphanes, the Jewish high priest Onias was replaced by his brother Jason, who hoped to turn Jerusalem into a Greek city, with a gymnasium and athletic games. But others wanted to go even further by introducing Greek-style worship as well. In 171 B.C., Menelaus bought the office of High Priest, removing the family of Jason and Onias, which had held this post by birthright. Civil war followed. Syria was again at war with Egypt, and Antiochus did not want this distraction in an important territory between the two countries. He tried to put down the rebellion but failed. He then decided that the solution was to crush the force that inspired Jewish opposition—the national religion and rituals. In 167 B.C., idols were placed in the Temple and unclean animals were sacrificed. Jewish rituals like circumcision and dietary laws were banned. In this Antiochus was supported by the extreme Greek sympathizers (called Hellenizers) among the Jews.

Pious Jews opposed Antiochus and the Hellenizers. But apparently they were poorly organized and were hunted down. According to 1 Maccabees, chapter 2, loyalty to the Sabbath was so great a thousand Jews chose to die rather than violate the Sabbath by fighting back against their attackers—an incident with echoes in one interpretation of the *Commentary on Habakkuk*. And 2 Maccabees is full of stories of martyrdom. Chapter 6, for example, tells the story of an aged scribe who is forced to eat swine's flesh in public. His tormentors say that he can eat whatever he wishes so long as he tells his followers that it is the forbidden food. He refuses, lest people be misled. With his dying breath he proclaims that God knows "I might have been delivered from death, but I am content to suffer these things." Another story of martyrdom (chapter 7) describes how a woman sees six of her seven children killed for refusing to eat swine. When the seventh is to be killed, she tells him, "My son, have pity upon me. Fear not this tormentor, but be worthy like your brothers and meet death."

Eventually, in the town of Modiin, the local priestly family headed by Mattathias called together the faithful with the cry, "Whoever is zealous for the law, follow me." Mattathias and his five sons led a rebellion. Judah, called Maccabee ("The Hammer"), emerged as a mighty warrior and clever strategist. In 164 B.C., his army captured the Temple in Jerusalem and rededicated it, establishing the festival of Hanukkah ("Dedication"), which is still observed by Jews. Religious liberty was restored, but the war against the Greeks and Hellenizers continued. Judah and two of his brothers fell in battle. Jonathan became high priest in 152 B.C. After his murder, Simon, the surviving brother, was named high priest and ruler in 140 B.C. Upon Simon's assassination, his son John Hyrcanus became high priest and later king, establishing the Hasmonean dynasty. Significantly, the Hasmonean kings adopted many aspects of Greek culture, to the displeasure of their pious followers. They also made many traditionalists angry by displacing the family of Zadok from the high priesthood and by accepting the crown, instead of placing a descendant of King David on the throne.

In discussing this period, the first-century Jewish historian Josephus introduces the three schools, or philosophies, of Judaism during the last centuries that the Second Temple stood in Jerusalem. The Sadducees take their name from Zadok, the high priest in the early days of the Davidic monarchy. While all those who supported the ancient right of Zadok's family against the takeover of the Hasmoneans might be considered Zadokites, the label *Sadducee* came to mean that part of the group representing the priestly class controlling the Temple and the aristocratic governing families. They demanded a strict reading of the Torah in making Jewish law. They also believed in free will and rejected the belief in angels and an afterlife as alien to the Torah.

The Pharisees—from Hebrew *perushim*—were "separatists." The name originally may have been an insult, but they turned it to their advantage by saying that they did indeed separate themselves—from the impurity and error of their enemies. They interpreted the Torah according to a tradition called the Oral Law, which they traced back to Moses and the revelation of the Ten Commandments at Mount Sinai. Using ideas that allowed for great flexibility and new ways, they looked for ways to apply the ancient laws to new and changing conditions. For example, they argued that the law of "an eye for an eye" referred to court-imposed fines, not physical revenge. And they found mention of angels and the immortality of the soul in the Bible. They united the belief in reward and punishment with an all-powerful deity by saying that while the result is already known, humans have free will along the way. Unlike hereditary priests, the Pharisees were laymen who earned authority on the basis of their scholarship.

Politically, they generally favored the common people and were supported by them in turn. The Talmud [a collection of Jewish law and traditions], whose rabbis considered themselves the spiritual heirs of the Pharisees, records the saying *(Pesaḥim* 57a): "Woe is me because of the House of Boethus.... Woe is me because of the House of Hanin.... Woe is me because of the House of Kathros.... Woe is me because of the House of Ishmael ben Phabi. Woe is me because of their fists. For they are High Priests and their sons are treasurers and their sons-in-law are trustees, and their servants beat the people with sticks." With the destruction of the Temple in 70 A.D., the priests and their Sadducean party lost significance, and the Judaism practiced by most Jews became identified with the Pharisees.

The Essenes were a smaller group that sought spiritual inspiration in prayer, extreme poverty, and isolation. They believed in angels, demons, the immortality of the soul, and an afterlife, as well as in an extreme form of predestination—the idea that everything has been determined since the beginning of time. Perhaps because of this, they did not preach in public or try to bring others into their sect, since the chosen were already known from the beginning of time. Pliny the Elder observes, however, that even though the Essenes forbid mating, the group continued to grow because unhappiness drove many converts to their home in the wilderness.

The Jewish philosopher Philo of Alexandria speaks also of the Therapeutae, or "healers," who resemble the Essenes in some ways. They gave up worldly possessions, devoted themselves to prayer, and ate as little as possible—some once a day, others once every several days. Two other groups of importance were the Zealots and the Sicarii. Josephus placed the Zealots in a fourth philosophy, or school; their defining characteristic was extreme nationalism and opposition to the Roman occupation. They refused to pay Roman taxes on religious grounds and called for the death of any Roman who entered the Temple. The Sicarii (from Greek *sikarioi*, "daggermen") were terrorists motivated by religious nationalism.

Despite appearances, however, very little was actually known about these groups because the sources of information about them were not entirely fair-minded in a modern historical sense. Josephus, who surrendered his command and went over to the Romans during the First Jewish Revolt (66-73 A.D.), paints the Zealots and the Sicarii in a very unsympathetic light. Both he and Philo, who wrote during the first half of the first century A.D., wanted to make Judaism respectable to Roman audiences. They therefore used a Hellenized—or Greek—framework that may have misrepresented Jewish thought by emphasizing philosophy and minimizing religious law.

Similarly suspicious for opposite reasons is the portrait of the Sadducees and the Pharisees found in the New Testament, where they serve as cardboard villains in their relationship to Jesus. The authors of the New Testament also wanted to make their message acceptable to the Hellenized world. Therefore, they may have focused on disagreements over ritual rather than politics and may have used Sadducees and Pharisees as safe substitutes for the Romans, who had life-and-death power and were the real mortal enemies of Jesus and his followers. It is worth noting, as Salo W. Baron pointed out in his monumental study, *A Social and Religious History of the Jews*, that almost all modern branches of Judaism claim spiritual descent from the Pharisees, no matter how they actually practice Judaism. In contrast, until recently most Christian writers accepted the negative picture of the Pharisees in the New Testament without analyzing the writers' reasons for showing them in that way. Many scrolls experts have expressed hope that evidence from the Dead Sea Scrolls will change these prejudices, but that remains uncertain.

Almost as soon as he read the *Manual of Discipline* in 1948, Eliezer Sukenik of the Hebrew University recognized the possibility that the document belonged to the Essenes described by Pliny the Elder in 77 A.D. In his *Natural History*, Pliny speaks of a group of Jewish men who lived near the west side of the Dead Sea, gave up sexual desire, shared their possessions, and had only palm trees as companions. Moving along to the next place in the survey, he says that *infra* this settlement is Ein Gedi. Taking the Latin word *infra*, or "below," to mean "south of," most scholars believe that Pliny places the Essenes between Ein Gedi, a well-known oasis, and the northwest tip of the Dead Sea. Qumran is the only ancient site found in this area, and since the scrolls came from a cave near this spot, the connection between the Essenes and the *Manual of Discipline* seems strong.

This connection becomes even more convincing when we note that the religion and its rules described in the *Manual of Discipline* and the *Damascus Document* resemble what Josephus and Philo say about the Essenes. In addition, two partial copies of the *Damascus Document* had been found by Professor Solomon Schechter in 1896 in the storage room of a synagogue in Old Cairo. The document spoke of a group of religious separatists who chose exile in Damascus to escape persecution. Schechter identified this group with the Karaites, a Jewish sect that rejects the law written by rabbis, accepting only the written Torah—*kara´* in Hebrew. When the originals of this work were discovered in the Qumran caves, however, it became clear that an earlier group had written the document. Again, the Essenes seemed to be a likely choice.

Josephus states that among the Essenes there were no extremes of wealth or poverty because they all shared what they had. The *Manual of Discipline* clearly requires the newly accepted member to hand over his property to the community. So, too, Josephus says that the Essenes ate their daily meal together after first ritually bathing, and this practice is shown in the manual. Moreover, the Essenes were especially concerned about purity and bodily functions. Josephus notes that the Essenes did not anoint their bodies because they considered oil to be a conductor of impurity. The *Damascus Document* seems to contain a similar view. As additional scrolls were discovered in the Qumran caves, they, too, appeared to reinforce the connection to the Essenes. The *Temple Scroll* and the *War Rule* both offer precise regulations for the placement and use of latrines, a concern that is consistent with what Josephus says about the Essenes. Finally, the Qumran scrolls take for granted the existence of angels and an afterlife, which were beliefs that Josephus and Philo say the Essenes had.

There are problems with this identification, however. Some beliefs and practices mentioned in the Qumran scrolls contradict what ancient authors said about the Essenes. Even more troublesome, the many Qumran documents do not always agree with each other. The Essenes are usually portrayed as not being interested in politics, living in isolation from the world. Yet fragment 4Q448 (document 448 from Qumran Cave 4) may praise "King Jonathan"—probably Alexander Janneus, whose name in Hebrew was Jonathan and who bore the title "king." In addition, while the *Manual of Discipline* requires new members to give their property to the community, the *Damascus Document* demands only two days' wages each month. Observers like Philo describe the Essenes as pacifists, but the *War Rule* is a very detailed battle plan for the final struggle between the Sons of Light and the Sons of Darkness. The Essenes often are said to be forbidden to marry, but the *Temple Scroll* specifically allows marrying a woman captured in war (similar to Deuteronomy 21:10-14). The official edition of 4Q502 labels it a "Ritual of Marriage" (though other scholars disagree), and the *Damascus Document* contains rules for families and condemns marrying more than one woman, but not marriage itself. This same document contains laws about the humane treatment of slaves, but the Essenes were said not to own slaves.

Those who believe that the Dead Sea Scrolls are the library of the Essenes explain these contradictions in a number of ways. First, they say that ancient authors may not have had firsthand knowledge of the Essenes. Pliny, for example, could not have visited all the places he describes and must have used information from other sources, perhaps some of it inaccurate. As for differences in the scrolls themselves, they cover a period of at least two centuries, during which time the beliefs of the group may have changed to accommodate a changed situation. Finally, the library certainly contained documents that were not written by the Essenes, like the hundreds of biblical texts. It is therefore possible that some documents that the group considered important enough to study may have contained ideas different from their own.

Opponents of this view change or reject the Essene connection. Some point out that *Essene* is almost an empty label, with only a few details filled in by ancient writers. Little is gained, they say, by insisting that the scrolls belonged to the Essenes. The group could more simply be called the Qumran sect or even the Dead Sea Scroll sect, if the connection between the caves and Khirbet Qumran is also questioned. Theodor H. Gaster, for example, argued almost from the publication of the first scrolls that the communities portrayed in the *Manual of Discipline* and the *Damascus Document* are ideals only and that such characters as the Teacher of Righteousness and the Wicked Priest were figures from Jewish history in general, not necessarily specific persons from the particular history of the Qumran sect. In his view, these documents may have been written before the sect and been adopted as models because they fit their particular circumstances. Since these texts belonged to the national religious literature available to all Jews, they could have influenced the practice of any number of untraditional groups, not just the Essenes.

Others believe that the scrolls give us a more accurate picture of the Essenes than the ancient writers do, including their growth and the conflicts that developed among them. In a number of works, Lawrence Schiffman argues that the Essenes began as Sadducees who disagreed with their leaders during the Hasmonean period in the second and first centuries B.C. In his account, the Sadducean, or Zadokite, high priest was displaced by a Hasmonean after the Maccabean victory, but the priests who officiated at the numerous sacrifices and

Temple rituals continued to be Sadducees. The Pharisees who protested the Hellenizing of John Hyrcanus and Alexander Janneus were persecuted and eventually rebelled. After their military victory in 89 B.C., the Pharisees made peace with Alexander Janneus and became the dominant party during the reign of his widow, Salome Alexandra. At this time, Schiffman believes, the Temple ritual was changed by the Pharisees, and, in protest, a group of Sadducean/Zadokite priests withdrew.

This would explain why the sectarians of the Dead Sea Scrolls refer to themselves as Sons of Zadok, obey a priest as their leader, and devote so much attention to ritual purity. In addition, some of the laws defended by the author of the *Halakhic Letter,* also known as MMT from *Miqṣat Maʿase ha-Torah,* "some rulings pertaining to the Torah," are attributed to the Sadducees by the Talmud. This does not mean that the scrolls were written by Sadducees, but it does explain the origin of the Qumran sect and the Essenes, if the two groups are the same. Those who reject Schiffman's ideas argue that the Sadducees and Essenes could have been different groups, which nonetheless agreed on some issues. In fact, being of conservative priestly backgrounds, both would have opposed Pharisaic innovations. But even more important, the religious beliefs of the Essenes—in angels, an afterlife, fate—is entirely contrary to Sadducean beliefs. This contrast cannot be attributed to anger over changes in Temple ritual.

Norman Golb explains the contradictions in the Dead Sea Scrolls by supposing that the caves did not contain the library of a Qumran sect or of any other single group. In fact, he believes that Qumran was a military base, not an Essene settlement. In this view, Pliny's use of *infra* does not place Ein Gedi "south of" the Essenes but, rather, "below" them in the mountains. As for the scrolls, in keeping with long-standing tradition, a number of people from Jerusalem hid their valuables in the Judean wilderness when the city was threatened with attack. This would explain why some of the caves are north of Qumran. Residents of Jerusalem, northwest of Qumran, might seek safe haven toward Jericho, to their east. In contrast, however, since the Roman army that attacked Qumran came from the north, Qumran residents would have hidden their belongings *south* of the settlement. Golb also points to the very large number of different handwritings in the scrolls—more than fifty in Cave 1 alone—as evidence that the scrolls were not written by the scribes of a small sect in a single settlement. Moreover, all the fragments found in Cave 7 are in Greek, again suggesting that they are a separate collection. Golb argues as well that all of the scrolls are copies, whereas one would expect to find at least some original manuscripts from such an educated and thriving community as Qumran is said to have been. In addition, none of the finds reflect the day-to-day operations of a community, such as records of income, inventories of food and supplies, personal letters, and the like.

Finally, the *Copper Scroll* demands an explanation. If the treasure is fictitious, the kind and purpose of the document are certainly unique among the scrolls. And if the wealth is real, it could not have belonged to a group of people living under vows of poverty. It must instead have represented the treasure of the Jerusalem Temple. Golb concludes that Qumran was not associated with the scrolls at all.

In opposing this idea, some argue that despite differences among the scrolls, they are surprisingly alike. The works that were found in multiple copies and in more than one cave reflect a distinct set of interests that may be called sectarian—belonging to one particular group of people. All the texts—books of the Bible, biblical commentaries, prayers, hymns, sectarian rituals—are religious in orientation. The scrolls contain no non-religious poetry, drama, history, or philosophy, and nothing practical about farming or the tending of animals. A few commercial documents were found in the caves, although Golb did not know about them because of the secrecy and delays in publication that surrounded the scrolls. Some experts also believe that the biblical commentaries are indeed original manuscripts, not professional copies. Finally, Golb's opponents find it unlikely that Pliny would mention only one settlement if two existed near each other; moreover, no sign of this second settlement has been unearthed.

Because Qumran was violently destroyed, probably in 68 A.D., some scholars believe that it must have been a stronghold of religious rebels who revolted against the Romans, such as the Zealots. They see no reason for the Roman army to attack and burn a settlement of peaceful people who lived in poverty. According to this view, the most important characteristics of the scrolls are a strict following of the law, a devotion to religious purity, and a hatred of outsiders. The best example of this attitude is in the *War Scroll,* with its blow-by-blow account of the preparations and battle plans for the final confrontation between the Sons of Light and the Sons of Darkness. Since some of the same texts were discovered at Qumran and Masada, known as the place of the rebels' last stand, supporters of this theory suggest that the two locations were part of a string of defenses, or that survivors of Qumran joined their colleagues at Masada for the final battle in 73 A.D. A form of the Zealot theory was proposed in the 1950s by the renowned Bible scholar Godfrey R. Driver and by Cecil Roth, an authority on Jewish history. These two especially attacked the early dating of the sectarian scrolls, arguing that paleography (the study of ancient written documents) could provide the order of when events happened, not their exact dates. They identified the Teacher of Righteousness with a Zealot leader and therefore dated the founding of the Qumran sect to the first century A.D. Against this explanation, scholars have pointed out that there is no evidence that the Zealots developed their own religion, shared property, or had the type of organization and communal life described in the scrolls. And as for questioning the destruction of a peaceful religious community, the Romans killed many innocent, peaceful people.

The late dating and connection to the Zealots also play a part in the idea proposed by Robert Eisenman. He believes that the scrolls reflect the political conflicts of the Holy Land in the first century A.D. According to Eisenman, Qumran was not a non-political pre-Christian "monastery" but a hotbed of extreme nationalism. After the Romans made Herod (a Jew) their puppet king (a ruler who seemed to be in power but was actually ruled himself by the Romans), Jews were divided over how to react. The Sadducees and Pharisees accepted foreign rule so long as religious practice was unaffected. But another group—called Zealots or Zadokites—fought to remove Roman paganism and leadership and was persecuted as a result. John the Baptist was a member of this movement, as was his cousin Jesus, who was executed as a revolutionary. Attaching names and faces to the vague titles in the Dead Sea Scrolls, Eisenman identifies the Teacher of Righteousness with James, the brother of Jesus, and the Man of Lies with Paul. He argues that the true meaning of the scrolls and of the New Testament has been made misleading by establishment interpretation. When they are liberated from these misleading ideas, Eisenman claims, they will clearly describe how the true Church of James the Just in Jerusalem was displaced by the false teachings of Paul to the Gentiles. Eisenman has charged that scrolls scholars dismiss his views and refuse to debate them. He sees this as additional proof that the establishment wants only to protect its turf.

Neil Asher Silberman says in *The Hidden Scrolls* that even though "many of Eisenman's proposed connections are based on intuitive leaps [guessing]...they offer an intriguing challenge to conventional wisdom." And Eisenman's ideas are popular among those who favor the idea of deceptions and conspiracies. Michael Baigent and Richard Leigh, for instance, give Eisenman center stage in their *The Dead Sea Scrolls Deception*.

Barbara Thiering is one of the authors who perceives a close connection between the Dead Sea Scrolls and early Christianity. In *Jesus and the Riddle of the Dead Sea Scrolls*, she argues that the Gospels and Acts are products of the Qumran sect. Although the surface text is full of miracles for those who need myths, a deeper, coded meaning lies beneath for those familiar with the sect's secrets. One of these secrets is *pesher*, or careful interpretation, a strategy used in Dead Sea texts like the commentaries on Habakkuk and Isaiah in order to apply ancient biblical verses to the sect. Thiering herself uses this technique on the Gospels and discovers that all the events that supposedly took place in Galilee and Jerusalem really occurred in the area of Qumran, including the birth and crucifixion of Jesus. She also finds that John the Baptist is the Teacher of Righteousness and Jesus is the Wicked Priest and that after faking his death, Jesus lived out his life in Rome along with his wife Mary Magdalene. This theory has almost no support among religious experts, although it caught the imagination of journalists and was the subject of a television documentary.

Any theory must account for the evidence. One theory is better than another to the degree that its explanation seems complete and sensible, and, if possible, simpler. The ruling view among scholars of the Dead Sea Scrolls is that they were written by the Essenes between the Hasmonean period of the last two centuries B.C. and the destruction of Qumran in 68 A.D. When the first scrolls were discovered, this seemed the simplest way to account for them. As more information has come to light, the theory has covered more ground but has become less simple. Even though different explanations have not achieved wide support, they highlight the need to keep examining the evidence. The mystery of the scrolls' authorship has not yet been fully solved.

CHAPTER 7

Monastery, Villa, Hotel—Or Fortress?

These days air-conditioned tourist buses leave Jerusalem daily and drive east along a well-maintained, paved highway to the northwestern shore of the Dead Sea, fifteen miles away. Here, at the lowest place on earth, 1,300 feet below sea level, another paved road along the western shore leads to a series of unique tourist attractions. Traveling south, tourists can visit the ruins in the archaeological park at Qumran, splash in the bracing waters of the oasis at Ein Gedi, or take the cable car from the snack bar at the foot of Masada to Herod's mountain palace-fortress at the summit. This place became the final stronghold of the Jewish rebels in the First Revolt against Rome and is now an archaeological park. A few miles farther south, vaca-tioners float on their backs in the Dead Sea—called the Salt Sea in Hebrew—whose salt content is so great that sinking is nearly impossible. After eating in the restaurant of the health spa next to the mineral baths, visitors return to Jerusalem for the evening.

During the 1950s, the situation here was very different. Qumran was on one side of the armistice line separating Israel and Jordan; Ein Gedi and Masada were on the other. Reaching Qumran from Jordanian-controlled East Jerusalem meant a winding, gut-wrenching jeep ride over a boring land-scape, a trip that only experts and a few Bible enthusiasts bothered to make. Getting to Masada from West Jerusalem, which lay at the eastern tip of Israeli territory poking into the Jordanian-occupied West Bank, involved hours of driving around the bulge of Jordan along narrow roads that twisted around the rocky hills and winding crevices of the Judean wilderness; or it meant leaving the bus that followed the main road toward Beersheba and the Negev and hiking the last few miles through blinding heat and choking dust.

Teenagers who climbed Masada—a rite of passage for many Israelis and Diaspora Jews who paid tribute to the stark memorial of ancient Jewish independence—would arrive exhausted and dust-caked the day before, camp out at the foot of the mountain, sometimes sharing a sleeping bag with a scorpion, and begin their ascent at sunrise, before the heat became unbearable. After an hour or so of climbing the nar-row snake path that clings to the eastern wall of the mountain, they would arrive at the summit, 1,300 feet above the Dead Sea, where they would eat breakfast amidst the ruins and mar-vel at the awesome vista across the valleys and hills on all sides. Then they would descend and continue on to the springs and mountain pools of Ein Gedi and the first bathing in days for many of the backpackers.

Hikers were struck by the emptiness and hostility of the landscape, the vast barren expanses broken suddenly by a thorny acacia tree or leafless broom. Low shrubs and bushes sprouted from the bed of a dried-up stream, waiting for a sud-den flood of water to wash down from the mountains to revive them. But the usual vegetation that sustains human life—

pastures, vineyards, groves, farms—was nowhere to be seen. Catching sight of an occasional solitary Bedouin walking along a dry river bed or across a distant hill was a source of wonderment: Where did he come from? Where was he going? How did he live out here? And one also thought of the thousands of slaves who had been worked to death carving the rock, carrying the lumber, digging the pools, bringing the furnishings, and supplying the daily food so that Herod could have his well-supplied vacation retreat on Masada to impress his Roman patrons with hot and cold baths and flowering gardens in this wasteland. It was this emptiness and isolation, some authors have suggested, that brought a band of Bedouin from the Ta'amireh clan here. Carrying illegal items and hoping to avoid the police on the road to Bethlehem, they chose to cross this wasteland and found themselves near the northwestern tip of the Dead Sea looking for a lost goat or resting in the shade near a cave that turned out to contain priceless scrolls hidden by some unknown persons long ago.

But where had these unknowns lived? Where in this unforgiving land could there have been a community with a library of this size, a community that, incredibly, wrote and studied books in this desert wilderness? Almost immediately after learning of the seven scrolls that had been found in a cave near the Dead Sea, G. Lankester Harding, Jordan's director of antiquities, set about locating and studying the cave. In February and March of 1949, he and Father Roland de Vaux of the École Biblique in Jerusalem led an excavation that turned up additional scroll fragments, as well as pieces of cloth and pottery similar to the type that protected the seven scrolls. Looking for the home of the people who had hidden the scrolls, they naturally suspected Khirbet Qumran ("the ruins of Qumran") about a mile to the south on a terrace between the hills to the west and the shore to the east.

After a quick search of the site, the two men dismissed it as a Roman fort, which is what it had been called by the German theologian and historian Gustav Dalman in 1914 and by the Jewish archaeologist Michael Avi-Yonah in 1940. In November and December 1951, they returned to Qumran for more careful study. This time they unearthed a jar and pottery similar to what they had found in the cave and concluded that the two sites were in fact used by the same people. After Bedouin discovered the manuscript-rich Cave 4 just a short walk from the ruins, de Vaux headed excavations at the site during four more campaigns, from 1953 to 1956.

Decent people would be horrified if a thief dug up their grandfather's grave to get at his gold watch. Yet they generally seem untroubled that explorers and museums have inflicted similar indignities on other cultures. The European explorers of the nineteenth century who brought back the treasures that still awe museum visitors had more in common with grave robbers than with modern archaeologists. They stole from ancient sites in their search for museum-quality exhibition pieces, looting the history of weaker peoples. When Napoleon's armies invaded Egypt in 1798, the scholars who accompanied them collected more than 100 statues and artifacts, including the Rosetta Stone, a monument covered with script in three languages that was the key to interpreting Egyptian hieroglyphics—an ancient form of writing. When the British defeated the French in Egypt in 1801, the treasures stored in Cairo were sent to France, but the collections in other cities were shipped to the British Museum, where the Rosetta Stone can still be viewed. Similar looting gave major European museums the Elgin Marbles, Assyrian temples, and Egyptian sphinxes. But like the Bedouin who ransacked the Dead Sea caves for scrolls, the European explorers simply discarded the broken pottery, fragments of cloth, broken weapons, and other "junk."

Toward the end of the century, William Flinders Petrie concluded that, for experts and historians, this junk was the most valuable part of a site. In particular, Petrie, who is considered the founder of scientific archaeology in Palestine, believed that the different layers, or strata, of settlement could be identified by the pottery found in each stratum. If an inhabited site was abandoned for a number of years, the mud brick would crumble and return to the earth. Or if war or natural disaster destroyed a settlement, the blowing soil and dust would soon bury even the remains of stone structures. In either case, the ground level would rise a few inches, and years later a new settlement might be built on top of the buried old one. Sometimes this process would be repeated several times to create an artificial hill or a tell. And if a trench were carefully dug, Petrie showed, these strata would be visible, the settlements where people lived getting older the lower one went.

In addition, Petrie argued that the key to dating each stratum was the pottery found in it. Dishes, bowls, cups, jars, and lamps are all-important to the archaeologist. Because earthenware, whether made from dried or fired clay, is inexpensive and breakable, new pottery was constantly being made, and so potters had plenty of chances to experiment with shapes and decorations. At any given moment, the pottery from a specific location is fairly consistent, but over time styles change. The shape of the rim, the placement of the handle, the curve of the side, the decoration and paint—all these are a matter of fashion and therefore mark a distinct period of time. Then, if a certain style of pottery is found in a stratum that also contains a datable coin or inscription, all other sites with similar pottery can be assigned the same date. Petrie also developed the technique of artifact "seriation," a process that assumes that changes happen in steps, meaning that similar styles are closer in time—in a series—than different styles.

Since changes in pottery, cloth, sandals, and weapons don't all occur at the same time, the mix of styles of various artifacts will help date a stratum—if the strata are excavated carefully and kept distinct. George A. Reisner, an American archaeologist who excavated at Samaria from 1908 to 1910, stressed the importance of daily reports, good records, maps, and photographs for separating strata. William Foxwell Albright, the most important biblical archaeologist in the 1930s and 1940s, combined archaeology, paleography, history, and knowledge of the Bible. He also refined the dating of pottery and developed a dated listing of styles—a typology—that is still used today. Starting in the 1930s, Sir Mortimer Wheeler and, later, his student Kathleen Kenyon created the Wheeler-Kenyon technique of digging within a grid of small squares that are defined by undisturbed walls of earth, called balks, which maintain a record of the strata.

In addition to the typology of pottery, other techniques since Petrie's day have been developed for dating finds and their associated strata. Experts are able to date cloth based on styles of stitching and sewing. The woven patterns' characteristics also point to the type of loom used in weaving. One method of dating that was still relatively new at the time of the Qumran dig is radiocarbon dating, also called the carbon 14 method. The normal atomic weight of the carbon atom is 12, but a tiny amount with an atomic weight of 14 also occurs naturally and is contained in the carbon dioxide that all living things absorb. When a plant or animal dies, the unstable carbon 14 starts to break up at a consistent rate. Measuring the amount of carbon 14 in linen or wood will show when the flax was picked or the tree cut down. More recently, an advanced form of carbon 14 dating called accelerator mass spectrometry has been applied to finds from Qumran. Because it requires very little material, it can be used even on scroll fragments.

When Harding and de Vaux explored Cave 1, the pottery and linen they found proved that this was the cave that had contained Mar Samuel's scrolls. When they then excavated Khirbet Qumran, the pottery and linen told them that this site was associated with the cave. In the five controlled excavations at Qumran, the goal was to expose and date the strata. Because exposing a lower stratum requires destroying the ones above it, maps are drawn, diagrams are made, photographs are taken, and detailed notes record the precise location of every find. Also, because the smallest fragment of pottery, cloth, bone, or metal is important, the tools of choice are fine picks, soft brushes, and sieves—not shovels and pickaxes.

The excavation of Qumran showed that the site had been lived in, abandoned, and returned to over a period of about 800 years. Pottery, an inscription in Phoenician letters, and a jar handle with a royal seal indicated that the walls of a rectangular building and a deep circular water tank dated to the eighth or seventh century B.C. This may have been the "city of Salt" in the wilderness, mentioned in Joshua 15:61-62. Or part of a military outpost from the reign of King Uzziah of Judah, who died about 740 B.C. and who, according to II Chronicles 26:10, "built towers in the desert and digged many wells." The site was again occupied during the Greek and Roman periods, which de Vaux divided into three phases.

In Phase Ia, which began about 130 B.C., at the start of the Hasmonean era, or possibly some years earlier, the circular water tank was repaired and two rectangular ones were added. A few rooms, as well as two pottery kilns, were built nearby. Beginning probably within a few years of 100 B.C., either at the end of the reign of John Hyrcanus or the start of the reign of Alexander Janneus, Phase Ib began with a building boom at the site. The settlement was enlarged to the west and south, second and third stories were added to existing buildings, and the three older water tanks were incorporated into an elaborate water system by which a dam captured the seasonal floods of Wadi (or River) Qumran and an aqueduct brought the water to reservoirs in the compound. This phase ended with a fire and an earthquake, in all likelihood the one that the first-century historian Josephus says occurred in 31 B.C. De Vaux believed that the site was uninhabited for about thirty-five years, when Phase II began. During this period the old buildings were repaired and reused. This phase ended with a great fire. The fire and Roman arrowheads in the ruins led de Vaux to date the destruction to 68 A.D., when the Romans attacked the settlement on their way to Jerusalem during the First Jewish Revolt. This was followed by Phase III, when the Romans built barracks and established a garrison at Qumran for about twenty years. The site was briefly used again during the Second Jewish Revolt of 132 to 135 A.D.

Hundreds of coins found at Qumran support these general dates. But exactly how to interpret them is a matter of debate. Three bowls containing more than 560 coins were discovered buried under a floor. The coins had images and inscriptions showing that they had been minted over a period of at least 120 years, from about 130 B.C. to about 10 B.C. By today's standards that is a very long time for coins to be in circulation. If all of these coins were in use at the same time, then finding a coin in an excavation does not pinpoint a precise date; it tells us only that a wall built on top of that layer must date to a time after the minting of the most recent coin. Thus, these coins indicate that Phase II began after 10 B.C. But whether they were used by the Qumran community or buried by someone else while the site was uninhabited is not clear.

Phase Ib was the main period of settlement activity. The compound, as defined by retaining walls and canals, was irregular in shape. The main structure is a large building complex about 100 feet by 120 feet, made of gray stone blocks, plastered inner walls, and pebbled floors. On its west side, this building connects, not quite at right angles, to the southeast end of an irregularly shaped north-south enclosure some 200 feet long by 100 feet wide, containing storerooms, pools, a water tank, and courtyards. A stone tower stands at the northwest corner of the main building where it adjoins the eastern line of the north-south enclosure. The tower consists of two stories of stone and possibly a third of brick. The outer walls of the tower are between 4 and 5 feet thick, and the inside was divided into a number of rooms that may have been used for storage or as prison cells. To the south of the tower, within the main building, is a large rectangular room that seems suitable for meetings, as well as rooms identified as a kitchen and laundry. Just south of this building, and separated from it by a large pool, is a long room, about 70 feet by 15 feet, that may have been a dining room. A pipe enters through a wall on one side and the floor slopes away; apparently water from this pipe washed food and dirt out the other end of the room. In an adjoining room more than a thousand dishes, bowls, and jugs were found stacked against the wall. To the east of these rooms were kilns and an area where all the pottery vessels might have been made. Other rooms served as a metal workshop, a flour mill, and a stable.

About 150 feet outside the eastern wall of the compound is a cemetery with more than a thousand graves arranged in parallel rows running north to south. Three smaller cemeteries are located nearby. Bodies were put directly into the graves, without coffins, ornamentation, possessions, or offerings. De Vaux opened about three dozen graves spread throughout the cemeteries. All of the identifiable remains in the main cemetery were male. In the extension or alternative cemeteries, skeletons of women and children were found as well.

De Vaux identified the Phase I and II settlements at Qumran with the community of Essenes that had been described by the Roman geographer Pliny the Elder and the Jewish historian Josephus. In his *Natural History*, written about 77 A.D., Pliny talks of a group of Jews living near the Dead Sea who had given up money, marriage, and the company of outsiders. Lying "below"—which de Vaux took to mean "south of"—the Essenes, Pliny says, is Ein Gedi, a desert oasis. Writing about twenty years later, Josephus tells his Roman audience that before the Temple in Jerusalem was destroyed, the Jews had three "philosophies" or schools of religious thought—the Pharisees, Sadducees, and Essenes. The Essenes are described in terms that we would now call monastic. De Vaux, being a Dominican priest, used the monastery as a helpful image, or metaphor, for explaining Qumran. As he studied the site, familiar concepts became labels for what he saw. He called the dining room the refectory, as it is called in monasteries. A large room with what looked like broken tables was the scriptorium, where the Qumran "monks" copied their scrolls. De Vaux labeled the many pools baptistries, or places where baptisms take place.

This Christianized version of Qumran became the official view of the International Team, and so it was often called a monastery and its Jewish inhabitants monks. Without necessarily using the same Christian terms, Eliezer Sukenik had also concluded that the scrolls were products of the Essenes. The *Damascus Document* speaks of the group being exiled in the wilderness, and the *Manual of Discipline* outlines a way of life marked by communal meals, ritual bathing, and, possibly, the avoidance of mating. The physical remains at Qumran certainly suggest a settlement organized on these principles. The large rooms would accommodate meetings, worship, and groups eating together. The many pools with steps could have been used for ritual bathing. And the great number of male skeletons in the cemeteries suggests a population of men without women. The association of the scrolls with the Essenes, and the identification of Qumran as their wilderness settlement, is accepted by most experts.

Not everyone believes that this explanation accounts for all the evidence. Based on the size of the cemetery and the seating capacity of the large rooms, the population of Qumran has been estimated at between 150 and 300. Missing from the buildings are living quarters for so many people. De Vaux and others suggested that the inhabitants met at the site for community activities like work, prayer, and fellowship but that they slept in tents outside the compound or in the caves. Opponents argue that the caves are too damp and dusty and that there is no evidence of the existence of tents. And where and how did the community get its food? There is no sign of farming near the settlement or on the surrounding land.

Edward M. Cook proposes that Qumran was an Essene purification center, not a settlement. The sectarian scrolls show a community that was very much concerned with ritual purity. Most Jews at that time believed that the Torah forbade the ritually impure from entering the Temple. But the scrolls extend the holiness of the Temple to the whole city of Jerusalem. Since corpses were impure, cemeteries had to be outside the city. And since corpses gave off impurity, whoever took part in the burial could not reenter the city for seven days. Dead animals also were impure, and leather from animals slaughtered outside the city could not be brought into Jerusalem. Thus, even scrolls written on parchment from the wrong source were a problem. Similarly, the emission of semen caused impurity for three days.

Either the Essenes had found it impossible to live in Jerusalem or they had found a way around the problem. Cook believes that for the Essenes of Jerusalem, Qumran, fifteen miles away, was the solution. The site offered large pools for ritual purification, and the buildings housed only a small permanent staff. Most of the people who ate in the dining room and met in the large halls were not permanent residents. And the large cemetery outside the compound was the final resting place for members of the Jerusalem fellowship.

More radical proposals entirely separate Qumran from the Essenes. One such approach comes, surprisingly, from scholars editing de Vaux's field notes. Though de Vaux shared his conclusions in many articles and lectures, he never published a final excavation report. In 1988 the École Biblique asked two Belgian scholars, Pauline Donceel-Voûte and Robert Donceel, to complete and issue the report. One defining characteristic of biblical archaeology has been the use of the Bible to help understand archaeology and of archaeology to interpret the Bible. If the ruin of an ancient city was discovered, the Bible was consulted in order to identify the city. If a musical instrument was dug up, it became the model for understanding David's harp. But Donceel-Voûte and Donceel specifically rejected using the scrolls to understand the dig. They insisted that the physical evidence had to speak for itself. And on this basis they announced that de Vaux was wrong. The site was not a religious center; it was a villa. Delicate glass, decorated bowls, elegant urns, and carved columns, they claimed, are more at home in a vacation retreat than in a monastery. And the many workshops were a common feature in rustic villas of the time. This idea has not convinced many experts. First of all, other villas from the time of Herod are much more elegant, with hot and cold baths, mosaic (elegantly decorated tile) floors, painted walls, and elaborate gardens. Also, while some fine tableware turned up at Qumran, the majority is simple, unadorned earthenware. Moreover, a family villa was not likely to have such a large cemetery.

Alan D. Crown and Lena Cansdale also argued that Qumran was not an Essene settlement. Hoping to avoid the objections to the villa theory, they believe that the site was an inn. They point out that in ancient times the Dead Sea was an important trade route, especially for spices, perfumes, and cosmetics coming to Jerusalem from Arabia and East Africa. The famous Madaba map—a mosaic in a sixth-century church in Madaba, Jordan—shows ships sailing on the Dead Sea. In fact, the high salt content that kept the sea "dead" of fish helped lift ships and allowed them to carry heavier loads than they could in other bodies of water. Crown and Cansdale believe that for a distance of perhaps 35 to 50 miles, this water route was much easier than a north-south trip along the rocky coast. And it was certainly more efficient for east-west travelers to cross the sea than to go around it.

In addition, the sea itself contained valuable minerals. Salt was harvested from the marshes at the south end, as was bitumen, a material used in paving roads, which may have been the object of a naval battle on the Dead Sea in 312 B.C. Crown and Cansdale see the Qumran buildings as a way station to accommodate travelers and protect the trade route. The large areas were dining rooms. The low tables that de Vaux believed were used for copying scrolls were actually couches on which guests lay down in the Roman fashion while dining. The tower provided protection. And the cemetery was for the many travelers who died during long trips.

Possibly the most extreme view is that Qumran was a fortress, protected by a strong tower and defense wall. This suggestion of Norman Golb's is part of his larger theory that the scrolls are from Jerusalem and that Qumran played a part in the revolt against Rome. Gustav Dalman and Michael Avi-Yonah had previously identified Qumran as a military fortress. It is widely accepted that the site was an Israelite fortress in the seventh century B.C. and a Roman garrison—or military fort—after the Jewish inhabitants were driven out in 68 A.D. This implies that the site had value for its position and, according to Golb, must have been a fortress all along. Pointing to the value of the mineral resources in the sea and the evidence of the Madaba map, he argues that Qumran was part of a series of fortifications that encircled Jerusalem.

At the beginning of the first century B.C., the Hasmonean ruler Alexander Janneus extended his kingdom east of the Dead Sea and built a fortress at Machaerus, about twelve miles southeast of Qumran on the facing shore. Golb notes that the two sites could have communicated by signal fire. Therefore Qumran was part of the line of forts known to have included Machaerus and was easily able to send reinforcements by boat in case of attack. Opponents of this view argue that the surrounding wall was not very thick or strong and had several entrances instead of a fortified gate. They also note that ancient farms and isolated settlements often had towers to warn against danger and that in this case the "tower" may have been no more than a two- or three-story building.

Finally, opponents of these differing views argue that their main weakness is the attempt to separate Qumran from the scrolls. In particular, Cave 4, where the largest collection of scrolls was found, is only a short walk from the ruins. The scrolls describe an isolated religious community especially concerned with ritual bathing. Nothing known about the site makes it unsuitable for such a group. However, it must be remembered that all of the findings of the excavations have yet to be published. De Vaux and his colleagues spread their own interpretation of the finds, but other experts are still waiting to see all the photographs, diagrams, and site reports. So it is possible that the existence of additional evidence may weaken the connection between Qumran and the scrolls. As Lawrence Schiffman—who accepts this connection—says in *Reclaiming the Dead Sea Scrolls*, "... until full publication of the excavation records and the records' reinvestigation by other scholars, the details of whatever we say here must to some extent remain tentative"—in other words, uncertain.

CHAPTER 8

Altering the Immutable Word

When the first Dead Sea Scrolls were discovered, the excitement centered on the ancient manuscript of Isaiah. After reviewing the photographs that John Trever had sent to him, William Foxwell Albright, the leading biblical archaeologist in America, called the *Isaiah Scroll* "the greatest manuscript discovery of modern times! . . . an absolutely incredible find." And when Yale University issued its press release in April 1948, the first paragraph focused on the "earliest known manuscript" of Isaiah, with the following paragraph giving only passing mention to the other three scrolls. Why was an old copy of a book from the Bible so important?

To appreciate the excitement over the biblical manuscripts among the Dead Sea Scrolls, we must understand how the Bible was read over the centuries. Although the general reader thinks of "the Bible" as an unchanging text—carved in stone, as it were—the issue is more complicated. At Qumran, as among Jews generally at the time, the Torah, Psalms, works of the prophets, and other holy texts existed as individual scrolls; they were not bound together in a single volume called the Bible. People considered certain scrolls sacred or inspired, but it is not clear whether they had a single label like *Bible* or *Holy*

Scripture that matched exactly with what we now call the Bible. Even a brief look will show that no two English translations of the Bible are the same. Many differences are nothing more than an editor's preference in vocabulary or sentence structure, but often the reason is that the translations are based on different ancient manuscripts.

For example, in the discussion of earthquakes in Chapter 1, we quoted from Zechariah 14:5, which in the Septuagint reads: "The valley of my mountains will be stopped up...and shall be stopped up as it was in the days of the earthquake in the reign of Uzziah king of Judah." But for the same verse, the King James Version has: "And ye shall flee to the valley of the mountains...like as ye fled from before the earthquake in the days of Uzziah king of Judah." A stopped-up valley in one version, fleeing citizens in the other. How can this be explained?

Hebrew, like other Semitic languages such as Arabic, builds almost all words (except, for example, pronouns and prepositions) on consonant roots, which do not occur alone as words. Rather, the roots, which usually contain three letters, provide a word field: *L-M-D* for "learning," *B-Q-R* for "examining," *K-T-B* for "writing." Before, after, and within these consonant roots, set combinations of vowels and consonants are attached to specify the exact meaning of the word: *me-a-e* for "one who," *a-a* for "he did." Thus, *meLaMeD* means "one who teaches"; *meBaQeR*, "one who examines"; *LaMaD*, "he learned"; and *KaTaB*, "he wrote." Ancient Hebrew spelling, again like Arabic and other Semitic languages, showed only consonants. But because most words had a consonantal prefix or suffix, the intended word was usually clear: *LMDT*, "you [sing.] learned"; *LMDTM*, "you [pl.] learned"; *YLMD*, "he will learn"; *NLMD*, "we will learn." The spelling was usually clear, but not always. Sometimes spelling was unclear because of the absence of the vowels that made words distinct in speech: *NSTM* could be understood as prefix *N* attached to root *STM*, or as *NS* with suffixed *TM*. In the first case the pronunciation is *nistam* and the meaning is "[it] was stopped up." In the second case the pronunciation is nastem and the meaning is "you [pl.] fled."

Similar disagreement over vowels accounts for a city in Genesis 10:10 that disappears from one translation to another. The King James Version assumes that *KLNH* is the name *kalneh* and reads: "And the beginning of his kingdom was Babel, and Erech, and Accad, and Calneh, in the land of Shinar." But the New English Bible reads *KLNH* as *kulanah*, or "all of them": "His kingdom in the beginning consisted of Babel, Erech, and Accad, all of them in the land of Shinar."

To aid in the correct pronunciation, a convention arose that indicated vowels by using certain "weak" consonant letters as *matres lectionis*, or "aids to reading": *h* for "a," *y* for "i," *w* for "o" and "u." Now *LMD (lamad)*, "he learned," would be visually distinct from *LMDH (lamda)*, "she learned," and *LMDW (lamdu)*, "they learned." A word spelled with these visual aids was said to be *plene*, or "full." Needless to say, *plene* spellings did not catch on with all scribes in all locations at the same time, so now they provide a means of recognizing different scribal (or writing) schools and traditions. In general, the Qumran scrolls use more *plene* spellings than does the style that became standard, but there was considerable variety even among these scrolls. Additionally, some *plene* spellings in the Dead Sea Scrolls imply a use of a local pronunciation that was unknown to experts before the discovery of the scrolls.

The almost-complete *Isaiah Scroll* published by the American Schools contains characteristic Qumranic forms as well as instances in which the scribe seems to have updated old-fashioned vocabulary and grammar. In a number of places this scroll contains alternative readings that some Bible experts consider superior to the accepted ones. Millar Burrows, who had studied the scroll in Jerusalem before returning to America, was a member of the translation committee for the Revised Standard Version (RSV) of the Bible. In 1948 he showed the group a list of such alternative readings; thirteen of them were incorporated into the text or mentioned in notes. For example, in the King James Version (KJV), the end of 33:8 is "he hath despised the cities, he regardeth no man." Instead of "cities," the *Isaiah Scroll* reads "witnesses," a difference in Hebrew between two similar-looking letters, *resh* in the first and *daleth* in the second. The RSV adopted the scroll reading. So, too, when verse 19:18 speaks of five Egyptian cities that will witness divine justice, the KJV ends with "one shall be called, The City of Destruction." The RSV, however, following the *Isaiah Scroll,* reads "City of the Sun," which looks like a translation of the Greek name "Heliopolis."

Of course, not all of the alternatives are equally attractive. Some seem to be attempts at simplification, and others may be errors. For example, in the King James Version, the last phrase of 3:24 is "burning instead of beauty," where "burning" translates the Hebrew *ky,* a rare noun. But there also is a common conjunction *ky* that means "because," and the copyist of the *Isaiah Scroll* seems to have felt that a word was missing from "because . . . instead of beauty." The scroll inserts "shame," and the RSV adopts this change: " . . . for shame shall take the place of beauty." However, the insertion is almost certainly an error because it ruins the structure and rhythm of the verse, which is a series of "this instead of that" phrases, with no conjunctions. Burrows himself later regretted some of the changes he had recommended, but they were retained in the New Revised Standard Version, and others were added. As additional Dead Sea Scroll texts have been published, to varying degrees other translations also have adopted alternative readings from the biblical scrolls.

It is worthwhile to consider why these different readings exist and why translators react to them differently. The Bible began as separate works by prophets, poets, philosophers, and historians. When a prophet like Isaiah or Amos announced his visions, someone wrote them down and circulated them. Jeremiah, for example, had a secretary named Baruch to record his words. Before these various writings were collected into a single book called the Bible, they circulated as separate scrolls of the type found in the Dead Sea caves. Because many people treasured the sacred scriptures, scribes copied them by hand over and over again. Long after the originals had fallen apart, copies of these important documents were copied, circulated, and studied. If a scribe made an error or updated the language or added an explanation, these were copied as well. In this way text "families" changed and grew. As time passed, the biblical books were translated, creating "versions" in Aramaic, Greek, Latin, and other languages. Occasionally, a scholar or religious body would carefully revise these texts, and the result would be new editions. These "recensions"—or revisions—would be copied and translated, starting the whole process over again. Thousands of manuscripts have survived to tell the story of this transmission over the centuries. The hundreds of biblical fragments among the Dead Sea Scrolls are important pieces of evidence of this written history.

The Hebrew text on which almost all translations of the Bible are based is called the Masoretic Text, a name derived from a verb meaning "to hand over, transmit." Tradition maintains that this text was transmitted from scribe to scribe, from generation to generation, in an unchanged form. But until the discovery of the Dead Sea Scrolls, the oldest Masoretic manuscripts dated only from the ninth and tenth centuries A.D. Although they were produced more than a thousand years after the individual books were composed, the best of these manuscripts, like the Aleppo Codex and others by the Ben Asher school of Tiberias, include a sophisticated and strict means for saving the accepted spelling, punctuation, and pronunciation. But what is "accepted" by tradition has long been regarded by scholars as suspicious. Logic insisted that so many scribes working over so many years had to make mistakes and change the text. In fact, the Masoretic Text differs in many places from other ancient "witnesses" such as the Greek Septuagint and the Samaritan Pentateuch and from quotations in the New Testament. These, in turn, sometimes agree with each other and sometimes do not, for each witness has its own history of being written and re-written. Debates have raged for centuries over which text represents the most accurate readings.

The original language of the Jewish scriptures was Hebrew, except for a few long passages in Ezra and Daniel that are in Aramaic, a related Semitic language. But after the Babylonian Exile, following the destruction of the southern kingdom of Judah in 586 B.C., Hebrew was not the language of daily life for many Jews. Because of conquest and economic influence, Aramaic was widely used throughout the Near East and remained the major political and commercial language even after Persia came to control the former empires of Babylonia and Assyria.

When Ezra returned from exile to Jerusalem in the middle of the fifth century B.C., he found that many Jews had intermarried with neighboring peoples and did not understand Hebrew. The book of Nehemiah (8:8) records that at a public ceremony marking the religious revival of Judea, Ezra read the Torah aloud and a translator explained it to the assembly. The very fact that Ezra and Daniel contain sections in Aramaic indicates that this was a common language among Jews of the time. In addition, the Jews replaced the ancient Hebrew script with the "square" Aramaic alphabet that is the source of the modern Hebrew writing system.

According to the traditional view, it was during this period that the schism—or division—of the Samaritans began. II Kings 17 tells how the northern kingdom of Israel, called Samaria, was conquered by the Assyrians in about 722 B.C. Under a policy of forced resettlement that was intended to destroy political and national unity, inhabitants of Samaria were exiled and their land given in turn to exiles from other countries. Since every land was thought to be protected by its local god, in typical Near Eastern fashion the foreign colonists added worship of the Jewish God to their religious practices. When the Persian government allowed Jews to return to Judea and rebuild the Temple, there already was an established Samaritan community. The narrative in Ezra and Nehemiah reports that the Samaritans wanted to help rebuild the Temple, but they were rejected. In anger, their leaders denounced the Jews as rebels to the Persian king, and the enmity between the two groups worsened.

The Samaritans themselves tell a different tale. They explain their name as coming from the Hebrew word *shomerim*, or "guardians," because they guarded the true religion of Israel. According to their Chronicles, they are the descendants of the Joseph tribes—Ephraim and Manasseh—and continuously lived in their ancestral land. Though they offered to help their returning co-religionists, they were rejected. After years of mistreatment, they were attacked by the Hasmonean king, John Hyrcanus, and in 128 B.C. their temple on Mount Gerizim was destroyed. While each version of the Samaritan story assigns the roles of hero and villain differently, both of them agree that by the second century B.C. the Samaritans had separated from the standard Judaism of the day. The Samaritan Bible is limited to the Pentateuch, or the Five Books of Moses, which is still written using a form of the ancient Hebrew alphabet.

While all of this was going on in Judea, a different story unfolded in Egypt, where many Jews, including the prophet Jeremiah, found safety after the destruction of the kingdom of Judah. When Alexander the Great conquered Egypt, he established Greek cities in an effort to unite his empire through a shared culture. The great metropolis of Alexandria attracted many Jews, who adopted the Greek language but kept the religion of their fathers. By the third century B.C., they needed a Greek translation of the sacred Hebrew scriptures. According to legend, seventy-two scholars from Jerusalem made the translation at the request of Ptolemy II Philadelphus in about

270 B.C.—hence the name Septuagint, from *Interpretatio Septuaginta Seniorum,* "Translation of the Seventy Elders," and the abbreviation LXX. While the original translation was limited to the Pentateuch, other books of the Bible were added over the years, as well as books that are not part of the Hebrew Bible such as Maccabees, Ben Sira, Judith, and Tobit. When Christianity spread to the Hellenized (Greek-influenced) world, the Greek Septuagint became the Old Testament of the Christian Bible. To this day, however, there remains disagreement as to the status of books that are not in the Hebrew Bible. Roman Catholics, for example, consider them part of the Old Testament, while Protestants make them a separate set of books called the Apocrypha.

There are, then, three major ancient biblical traditions, each sacred to a different religion: the Masoretic Text to Judaism, the Samaritan Pentateuch to the Samaritans, and the Septuagint to Christianity. Each religion naturally assumes the superiority of its version over the others in the numerous conflicting readings that exist.

Some variations may arise in several different ways—through errors, editing, and tampering by those with a particular argument to promote, for example. A scribe may omit letters or words if his eye jumps from the word he is copying to one that is similar later in the passage. In the Septuagint, 1 Samuel 14:41 reads: "Saul said to the Lord, 'God of Israel, Why have you not responded to your servant today? If the iniquity was due to my son Jonathan or to me, Lord, God of Israel, let the lot show Urim; and if you say it was due to your people Israel, let it show Thummim.'" In contrast, the Hebrew text omits everything between the first and last occurrences of the word *Israel*: "Saul said to the Lord, 'God of Israel, Let it show Thummim.'"

Sometimes changes are deliberate. Copyists often took the liberty of correcting a text or adding something to make it clearer. We have already noted that Qumran texts contain updated language and grammar. Jewish tradition also speaks of *tiqqun sopherim*, "scribal emendation" or correction of disrespectful or misleading phrases. For example, tradition says that in Genesis 18:22 "Abraham stood before the Lord" replaced the phrase "the Lord stood before Abraham" so as not to imply that God was serving Abraham. So, too, in 1 Kings 21:10 and 13 the substitution "bless God" is written instead of the unacceptable "curse God." Significantly, the Talmud (Sopherim I, 8) defends changes that it says the translators of the Septuagint introduced in order to make the Bible more understandable and acceptable to a Greek-speaking audience.

It has been long argued that many, if not most, of the variants in the Septuagint could be traced to errors in translation. Certainly, some show a misunderstanding of Hebrew poetic technique. The Masoretic Text of Zechariah 9:9 reads: "Rejoice greatly, daughter of Zion; shout, daughter of Jerusalem. Behold, your king is coming to you; he is just and triumphant, humble and riding on an ass, upon the foal of an ass." Here, each unit is reinforced by two words that mean either the same thing or a parallel: rejoice/shout, Zion/Jerusalem, just and triumphant/humble and riding. But the translators of the Septuagint apparently missed the parallel between ass/foal of an ass and instead pictured two animals— an ass and a foal. This error—if that's what it is—is significant because the verse is used as a proof-text in Matthew 21:2-7—

"to fulfill the words of the prophet"—where Jesus seems to ride into Jerusalem on both the ass and the foal at the same time.

What looks like a similar error in Isaiah 40:3 may actually be a deliberate "creative misreading." Almost all modern Bible scholars recognize parallel phrases in the Hebrew: "A voice cries out, 'In the wilderness prepare the way of the Lord, in the desert make straight a highway for our God.'" The Septuagint, however, reads: "A voice of one crying in the wilderness, 'Prepare the way of the Lord....'" While it gives the scholarly version in the text, the Jerusalem Bible, a modern Catholic translation, explains in a note that the evangelists quote the Septuagint version because they understood it to predict John the Baptist.

One goal of textual work has been to get behind the changes and errors to recover the original Bible, the "true" Bible. Until the discovery of the Dead Sea Scrolls, this involved mostly educated guesses based on late manuscripts and ancient witnesses. In some cases, an insightful correction by a modern editor was later found in a scroll. Based on the Masoretic Text, the famous vision in Isaiah 11:6 traditionally reads: "The wolf shall dwell with the lamb, and the leopard shall lie down with the kid; and the calf and the young lion and the fatling together; and a little child shall lead them." Given the parallels between the phrases, we would expect a verb instead of "the fatling" and, in fact, a slight change in the Hebrew letters yields "will feed": "the calf and the young lion will feed together." This reading is in the *Isaiah Scroll* and seems superior to the traditional Masoretic reading.

In addition, there are Hebrew texts among the Dead Sea Scrolls that seem to underlie readings in the Septuagint and the Samaritan Pentateuch that differ from the Masoretic Text. Estimates vary because of the difficulty in assigning some fragments. One accepted view is that 60 percent belong to the Masoretic group, 5 percent to the Septuagint, 5 percent to the Samaritan, 20 percent to a unique Qumranic type, with 10 percent being "nonaligned," or not belonging to any of the groups. Evidence from the large number of Masoretic scrolls illustrates how carefully this text was preserved. But finding ancient Hebrew manuscripts that support other readings proves that these are variants of long standing, not simply errors in later versions.

Of course, just because something is ancient does not necessarily mean that it is the true, original version. We have already seen that ancient editors tried to correct difficult texts. Bible scholars use techniques from literary criticism to identify such corrections. Psalm 145 is an alphabetical acrostic—the first letter of each line spells out the alphabet. For example, the first line begins with *aleph* (A), the second with *beth* (B), and so on through the alphabet, except that in the Masoretic Text there is no line for *nun* (N). Some English translations followed the Greek when supplying the missing line. Now it has been found in a scroll from Cave 11. Is it original? Many experts believe that it is not original because it uses the divine name Elohim instead of YHWH, as in the rest of the poem. Nonetheless, knowing that the ancient version has a respectable pedigree gives scholars added confidence when the Hebrew is difficult or obviously in error.

The special Qumran type offers some intriguing readings. Scholars have long felt that the Masoretic Text of 1 Samuel creates a problem because some items have been left out or repeated apparently for no reason. One apparent omission occurs in 11:1, which begins, "Nahash the Ammonite came and besieged Jabesh-gilead...." Nahash is not introduced in the usual style—Nahash, *King of the Ammonites*—and there is no explanation for the Ammonite attack. But in one of the Samuel scrolls from Cave 4, two additional sentences stand before this, beginning with the expected "Nahash, king of the Ammonites" and describing how 7,000 of his enemies had found safe haven in Jabesh-gilead. Unlike many other additions in Qumran scrolls, which read like lines added for clarity by later copyists, this one is accepted by most Bible experts as part of the original. The New Revised Standard Version (NRSV) includes it in the text, and other translations mention it in a note. Having thus accepted the superiority of the Samuel Scroll, some translators use other variants as well. According to Harold Scanlin, in *The Dead Sea Scrolls and Modern Translations of the Old Testament*, the NRSV translation of 1 Samuel adopts 110 alternatives to the Masoretic Text, the New English Bible, 160, and the New American Bible, 230.

Evidence from the scrolls also promises a better understanding of how the Bible was standardized and spread from one group of people to another. Frank Moore Cross, a member of the original International Team who had responsibility for the biblical material, concludes that three distinct text types existed in Palestine, Egypt, and Babylonia. The earliest sections of the Bible were composed in the kingdoms of Judah and Israel. The Jews who settled in Babylonia and Egypt after the destruction of their land took with them copies of sacred writings. During the years when Jews were sent to other lands and isolated from each other, different changes occurred in the scriptures of the three communities. The Palestinian family is represented by the Samaritan Pentateuch, the Egyptian by the Septuagint, and the Babylonian by the Masoretic Text. Cross believes that the small-scale return of Jews under Ezra to the Persian province of Judea was followed by a mass return to the newly independent homeland after the Maccabean victory.

Three differing versions of Holy Writ now coexisted in Judea. When religious disputes arose among the Pharisees, Sadducees, and Essenes, it became essential to have a single text that all would accept. This took time, as we can see by comparing the early manuscripts from Qumran with the later ones from Masada, Wadi Murabba'at, and Nahal Hever. Cross argues that adoption of the Babylonian type as the standard probably occurred before the end of the first century A.D. and certainly by the time of the Bar-Kokhba rebellion in the years 132 to 135.

However, not all scholars accept Cross's ideas about the three territorially identified families or about the date of standardization. Some point out, for example, that the Dead Sea Scrolls show more than three text types, and they suggest that Cross supposes that there were three locales because he is already taking for granted an explanation for the Samaritan, Septuagint, and Masoretic texts. But there is general agreement that the Masoretic Text was firmly established no later than the time of Bar-Kokhba. The Greek version of the Minor Prophets found at Nahal Hever shows evidence of an attempt to edit a translation based on the Septuagint so that it would agree with the Masoretic Text.

Another type of written bible history investigates what is called "canon"—that is, which texts are held sacred by specific faith communities at any given time and how they are understood. We have the books of the Hebrew Bible because Jews valued, studied, and preserved them. Yet Numbers 21:14-15 quotes from the now-lost Book of the Wars of the Lord. And 1 and 2 Kings repeatedly tell the reader that additional information can be found in the royal chronicles of Judah and Israel, which no longer exist.

The scrolls from the Qumran caves contribute to the study of the biblical canon in a number of ways. To begin with, they contain at least fragments of all the books of the Hebrew Bible except Esther (although an "Esther-like" text is represented). And if a book's importance can be judged by how many copies of it are in the library, we could conclude that the Qumran sect revered the books of the Torah because their library held eighteen copies of Genesis and Exodus, seventeen of Leviticus, twelve of Numbers, thirty-one of Deuteronomy, thirty-nine of Psalms, and twenty-two of Isaiah. But the Qumran scrolls also include fifteen copies of Jubilees and eleven of Enoch, more than any of the remaining books of the Hebrew Bible. Even the short story Tobit, with five copies, would seem to have been more important to them than Song of Songs, Ruth, and Lamentations (four each), or Joshua, Proverbs, and Ecclesiastes (two each). Finally, the works of biblical interpretation called *pesharim* are especially valuable in showing us which works this group of Jews considered inspired and how they understood the significance of the Bible in the world, their community, and their personal lives.

The Qumran evidence must be used carefully, however, since the larger significance of the scrolls can be overstated. If the scrolls represent the library of the Qumran sect, as most scholars believe they do, then they tell us only about this breakaway sect, not about Judaism in general. The sectarian scrolls portray a group that rejected the Jerusalem Temple as well as the general religion of the nation and the practices of the popular religious parties. Their fascination with Isaiah, Jubilees, and Enoch tells us about their interests, but not about what was considered Holy Writ for mainstream Judaism or even other sects. Likewise, the fact that they were untroubled by multiple versions of sacred texts does not mean that this attitude was the norm.

As for the role of the scrolls in recovering the original text of the Bible, again care is in order. The fragments of most of the books are only a small fraction of the full text, sometimes only a few sentences. Although copies of Samuel, Isaiah, and Jeremiah offer areas for comparison, many of the other fragments are tiny and lack context. They may not be biblical texts at all but rather rewordings in commentaries or prayers. As such they are not evidence of different readings. Even large fragments present such problems. The *Psalms Scroll* from Cave 11 contains a selection of psalms, mostly from the last third of the book, and a few additional works. James A. Sanders, the editor, maintains that differences in content and order between this fragment and the traditional text prove that alternative psalm books existed as late as the first century A.D. But opponents of this view note that the differences—taken together with the nature of the additions—could also prove that these forty-one psalms were part of a prayer book, not a biblical scroll.

Nonetheless, the scrolls prove that versions such as the Septuagint and the Samaritan Pentateuch are ancient and may preserve accurate readings. The Hebrew Old Testament Text Project tries to evaluate the evidence and offer advice to translators. But in the end, each editor must decide what weight to give ancient manuscripts. The New Jewish Publication Society translation claims simply to follow the traditional Masoretic Text. On the other hand, the New English Bible, treats the Masoretic Text almost with disrespect, saying in the preface that it is "full of errors of every kind, due to defective archetypes...confusion of letters, omissions and insertions...." This translation incorporates so many readings from the Septuagint, the Dead Sea Scrolls, and other witnesses that the editorial committee issued a separate booklet called *The Hebrew Text of the Old Testament: The Readings Adopted by the Translators of the New English Bible.*

Finally, at a conference in Jerusalem in July 1997, celebrating the fiftieth anniversary of the Cave 1 finds, a number of participants, including Emmanuel Tov, chief editor of the publication committee, called for a new, critical text of the Hebrew Bible, based on the Dead Sea Scrolls. Others opposed the idea, saying that those who revere the Bible consider the existing text sacred.

CHAPTER 9

ᴄThe Scrolls, ᴄReligion, and Conspiracy

Among the many mysteries that surround the Dead Sea Scrolls, one of the most puzzling is: Why the delay in publication? The first of the Dead Sea Scrolls were discovered in 1947 and were greeted by the public with much excitement. Photographs were quickly released and edited versions appeared within a few years. Experts of all religions and nationalities were thus able to study these documents and use the information in their histories of Judaism and Christianity.

But the hundreds of manuscripts that were discovered during the major searches of the Judean desert over the next few years were not so quickly released. Nor were many of them available even in photographs to experts outside the official team of editors. Periodically an editor would mention in an article or at a convention that he had found an important passage—one that might even justify major revisions in histories of early Judaism and Christianity. But the rest of the world had only the editor's word for this. The document could not be checked until the complete edited version was published—always "sometime in the near future." But the near future frequently did not arrive, and the scrolls therefore remained unavailable.

It is possible that the work was simply too much for the team of editors. The first scrolls that were discovered and published were, by and large, whole. And sometimes when the beginning or end was missing, or when the bottom of a column was shredded, large sections of text remained. With the later discoveries, a "scroll" might be represented by nothing more than dozens of fragments, mixed together with thousands of other, unrelated fragments. Assembling this massive collection of jigsaw puzzles might have been overwhelming.

Nevertheless, some critics did not accept such an innocent explanation. If the job is too big, they argued, call in additional help. Don't allow a small group to deny the scrolls to the rest of the world. No, they said, the explanation must lie in a deliberate conspiracy, a plot to hide the earthshaking revelations of the scrolls.

Almost from the beginning, excitement over the scrolls in some quarters was matched by fear in others. Even as experts wondered how the scrolls could contribute to our knowledge of the Bible and early Christianity, some devout Christians feared that these findings would question Christianity's claims to its unique and miraculous origins. When A. Powell Davies, pastor of All Souls Church in Washington, D.C., published *The Meaning of the Dead Sea Scrolls* in 1956, one of his goals seems to have been to ease these fears. After reviewing the then-current scrolls study and the challenge to Christianity, Davies wrote, "It is felt by many, especially among the clergy, that the new discoveries must be met with hostility and their effect minimized." And he asks: "Must churches always be defensive? Surely they must sometime recognize that God can work through natural events in a gradual social evolution."

Yet fears were stoked by sensationalist public statements by John Allegro, one of the members of the International Team. Allegro had studied to be a Methodist minister and had received a scholarship to Oxford University, where he pursued advanced work in Hebrew. While still in graduate school, he was recommended for appointment to the editorial team working on the scrolls at the École Biblique in Jordanian East Jerusalem. By this time, however, he had apparently lost his faith and seems to have taken pleasure in teasing his devout Catholic and Protestant colleagues at the École. At one point he is reported to have teased fellow-editor John Strugnell, an Anglican who also took comfort in Catholicism, by saying: "...by the time I've finished there won't be any Church left for you to join." The journalist and critic Edmund Wilson, who met Allegro in Jerusalem, describes him as "irreverent and rather brash," a member of "the species of what was then called the Angry Young Men."

Allegro also had a flair for the dramatic and an appetite for publicity. Before he published the Nahum commentary (or *pesher*) that had been assigned to him, he announced on British radio that this scroll described how the Wicked Priest, identified as Alexander Janneus, had crucified the Teacher of Righteousness and how the Qumran sect was guarding the Teacher's body until Judgment Day. Although he drew attention to the parallel between this story and the later Gospel account of Jesus, his official publication of the fragment showed that most of the identifications and narrative were colorful guesses and made-up stories, complete with invented scenes. In a later essay he argued that the Gospels were written by Essenes and that all the characters—including Jesus—

were myths or coded references to sect members. Finally, Allegro self-destructed with his publication of *The Sacred Mushroom and the Cross*, which claims, in the spirit of the Age of Aquarius, that Christianity began as a mystery/fertility cult in which members used drugs derived from mushrooms to induce visions and psychic experiences.

In response to Allegro's earliest wild statements, Father Roland de Vaux, head of the International Team, and four other members issued a letter to the press saying that nothing they had seen in the scrolls supported Allegro's version of Essene history and its foreshadowing of Christianity. Then Father Geoffrey Graystone issued a series of articles in Catholic periodicals playing down any connection between the Qumran sect and Christianity, and, in contrast, emphasized the many differences between the two. Interestingly, he also implied that all was well because there were a large number of Catholics on the editorial committee and because the Vatican was a sponsor, having participated in G. Lankester Harding's program for foreign institutions to purchase scrolls. In a separate work, *The Dead Sea Scrolls and the Originality of Christ*, Father Graystone took aim at Edmund Wilson as well.

A great deal of the early popular interest in the Dead Sea Scrolls has been credited to Wilson, a politically left-leaning journalist and literary critic. In 1955 he published a short book entitled *The Scrolls from the Dead Sea*, which expanded on a piece he had written for the *New Yorker*, a magazine targeted at sophisticated and well-read general readers. The essay told the story of how the first scrolls were discovered by Bedouin, and it introduced readers to Mar Samuel, the Essenes, and Qumran. Wilson then surveyed what he called the "tension" surrounding discussion of the scrolls, which he claimed arose from "other anxieties than the purely scholarly ones." Based on interviews in Jerusalem with members of the International Team and other scholars familiar with the already published scrolls, Wilson noticed "a certain reluctance" on the part of Christians to accept the idea that central Christian beliefs had come about "gradually and naturally" over a few centuries from the doctrines of a sect of Jewish dissidents.

In support of this Christian dependence on Jewish sources, Wilson outlined the view of André Dupont-Sommer, professor of Semitic Languages and Civilizations at the Sorbonne in Paris. Dupont-Sommer argued that the Essene sect "heralds and prepares the way for" Christianity. The Essenes revered a Teacher of Righteousness who preached poverty and chastity, was thought to be a savior, was persecuted and killed, and who would return as supreme judge at the end of time. Since, by Dupont-Sommer's reckoning, the Teacher of Righteousness died half a century before Jesus was born, similarities between the two were the result of Christian "borrowing." Although Wilson wrote that Dupont-Sommer "over-played his hand" and interpreted the scrolls too freely, he nonetheless concluded that the message of the scrolls was positive: ". . . it would seem an immense advantage . . . that the rise of Christianity should, at last, be generally understood as simply an episode of human history rather than propagated [spread] as dogma and divine revelation."

In 1967 the *New Yorker* sent Wilson back to Jerusalem to bring his report of the scrolls up-to-date. His later reports were then attached to his earlier book and, together with another essay, were published as *Israel and the Dead Sea Scrolls*.

This work includes a section labeled "Polemics," which gives an overview of reactions to his original book, including the reaction of Father Geoffrey Graystone. Edmund Wilson characterizes Graystone's book as "a simple piece of Catholic apologetics...without acrimony, in a tone of patient good will." This he contrasts with other reviews that exhibited a "complete lack of scruple" in misrepresenting his views and biblical scholarship to an uninformed lay (non-clergy) audience. Wilson also notes that Catholic scholars know a great deal more about comparative religion than they have shared with lay people. Therefore, while Dupont-Sommer's professional articles could be passed over in silence, Wilson's own popular essays had to be countered because what the Catholic Church really wanted to do was to minimize the importance of the scrolls.

This is the charge at the heart of the conspiracy theory presented by Michael Baigent and Richard Leigh in *The Dead Sea Scrolls Deception*. "One is compelled to ask," they write, whether something more than the reputation of individuals is at stake—"the vested interest of Christianity as a whole, for example, and of Christian doctrine...." Baigent and Leigh weave their web of conspiracy from many threads. They begin with the seemingly innocent fact that despite the early excitement over the scrolls, within a few years public interest had died down. As they see it, however, this early interest was unwelcome and had been "skillfully defused." The official view seemed to be that everything worth knowing about the scrolls was now known and was "less dramatic than had been expected." But how could this be, if so much of the find had not yet been interpreted? According to Baigent and Leigh, enough had been uncovered to shake the very foundations of orthodox Christianity and to undermine accepted beliefs about Jesus, Paul, and the uniqueness of Christian theology. And it was this that the editors of the scrolls were hiding.

Ironically, one of the very things that Father Graystone had offered as comfort for his Catholic audience became a source of suspicion to Baigent and Leigh. They charge that the editing team seemed to be heavily weighted with Catholic priests and others loyal to the Vatican: Father Roland de Vaux (head of the group), Father Patrick Skehan, Father Jean Starcky, Father Jozef Milik, Father Maurice Baillet, and Professor John Strugnell, a convert to Catholicism. The church's "high-level involvement" was cause for suspicion, Baigent and Leigh claimed. "Can one ignore the possibility of a causal connection between that involvement and the shambles that Qumran research has become?" Moreover, the work was sponsored by the École Biblique, which answered to the Pontifical Biblical Commission, which in turn was controlled by the Congregation for the Doctrine of the Faith.

Baigent and Leigh were especially troubled by the congregation's published view that "the freedom of the act of faith cannot justify a right to dissent," or disagree with the church. To them this meant that for a professing Catholic scholar, the search for truth must be less important than the teachings of the church. They found it "profoundly disturbing" that, in light of this statement, all information about the Qumran texts from the official editing team "will be subject to the censorship machinery of the Congregation."

Why are the Dead Sea Scrolls considered so dangerous? All biblical scholars agree that the existing texts of the New

Testament were selected from a larger body of stories, memoirs, and letters; and most agree that these texts contain little, if any, eyewitness information about Jesus. The Gospels were composed at least a generation after the death of Jesus; and Paul, the author of the great theological epistles, does not claim to have met Jesus in the flesh. This suggests to many scholars that what we have in the New Testament is not a clear, simple collection of observations of and reactions to Jesus, but, rather, a carefully crafted official version of the history of the Jesus movement.

The Dead Sea Scrolls, however, are different. They were hidden away and forgotten. Like a time capsule, they were frozen in their eternal present—untouched, unchanged, unedited. The original public fascination with the scrolls must have come from this sense that they were "really there." These very pieces of parchment and papyrus might have been held by Jesus or John the Baptist. If there were personal letters among the scrolls, they might mention Jesus or one of the apostles. If there were stories, they might be eyewitness accounts. Whatever was in these documents, at the very least it would tell us what real people said and thought and did during the years immediately before and after the time of Jesus. Who could even imagine what we might discover?

And this, charge Baigent and Leigh, was the problem: "Might they contain something compromising, something that challenges, possibly even refutes, established traditions?" Could Allegro have been telling the truth when he teased Strugnell about destroying the church? To avoid this possibility, they suggest, the official scrolls team forced all evidence into the most innocent and harmless interpretation—and may have withheld damaging evidence. Baigent and Leigh label the official interpretation the "consensus" view and argue that it was harmless because it distanced the scrolls from the origins of Christianity. The scrolls were said to date from at least a century or two before the Christian era and to reflect the beliefs of a small sect, perhaps during the Maccabean period. Thus, Jesus and his followers could not have been influenced by the scrolls that spoke of an anointed one (or "Messiah"), a Teacher of Righteousness, and a Wicked Priest who persecuted him, nor by those who preached an extreme nationalism. Mainstream Judaism remained as it is pictured in the New Testament, and Christianity remained something unique.

The truth, however, say Baigent and Leigh, is that the beliefs of early Christianity closely resembled those described in the scrolls: Both groups practiced baptism, both did not believe in owning private property, both were organized around a Council of Twelve, and both believed that a Messiah would come. And what's more, Baigent and Leigh claimed, the correct interpretation of the Dead Sea Scrolls is the one proposed by Robert Eisenman: James the Just, the brother of Jesus, was the true leader of the early Church until he was overthrown and written out of history by a traitor—Paul. This, say Baigent and Leigh, is what the Dead Sea Scrolls threatened to tell and what the team of editors suppressed.

But is it so? Hershel Shanks, editor of the *Biblical Archaeology Review,* thinks it isn't. In fact, in a review reprinted in his book *Understanding the Dead Sea Scrolls,* he calls the charges "hogwash" and "ludicrous." Concerning the charge that Catholic experts are censored by the Vatican, Shanks (a non-Catholic) answers that they are, rather, "in the forefront of modern critical biblical scholarship," sponsoring such respected journals as the *Catholic Biblical Quarterly* and *Revue Biblique*, the latter published by the École Biblique.

Moreover, three of the most vocal critics of the consensus view and of the official editing team are Catholic priests: Father Joseph Fitzmyer of the Catholic University in Washington, D.C. (who, it might be added, in 1974 published the "Son of God" text from Qumran Cave 4); Father Robert North of the Pontifical Biblical Institute in Rome; and Father José O'Callaghan, a Spanish Jesuit who claims that Qumran Cave 7 contained fragments of the New Testament. "No one," says Shanks, "can deny all these dissenting scholars a voice." This last point is not entirely convincing since Shanks admits that dissenters could be denied a hearing at meetings that the editorial team controlled. That, after all, is the heart of Baigent and Leigh's accusation. Even they do not contend that the official team and the Vatican can control every conference everywhere, although they do see Vatican power influencing more than just official meetings.

When he takes on the substance of their attack on the consensus view, however, Shanks offers a strong argument against Baigent and Leigh. They argue that the official team attempted to protect the uniqueness of Christianity by dating the scrolls to a century or two before the time of Jesus. But, as Shanks correctly notes, this does not accomplish anything. If a scroll dating from a century before Christianity speaks of a virgin birth or of a crucified Messiah, this can hardly protect the special story of Christianity. On the contrary, it suggests that basic beliefs of Christianity were held by Jews generations before Jesus was born and could have been adapted by the

Jesus movement, not revealed as a new covenant. But we have known this for years. As Shanks says, virgin birth stories are known in the myths and stories of many religions, just as Mesopotamian flood stories existed before the biblical story of Noah. And still Christianity has not crumbled. The reason for the inexcusable delay in publication, says Shanks, was power. The scholars who controlled the scrolls controlled the field. Their names would live forever. They would attract the good graduate students. It was nothing more sinister than human weakness, says Shanks, that led to this scandal.

Of course, one of the keys to success for a conspiracy is that it be secret. Therefore, an outsider cannot say beyond question that none exists. But one can say that Baigent and Leigh do not make a convincing case. Their accusations read like a certain type of anti-Catholic fear. There are those who believe that the Catholic Church today is still the church of the Spanish Inquisition, or the church that forced Galileo to deny his ideas about the solar system. And there are certainly those who see Catholic plots everywhere. But too much of Baigent and Leigh's case is based on vague accusations and quotes that are taken out of their original context.

In one particularly annoying example, they speak of the widespread agreement that "the history of Dead Sea Scroll scholarship does constitute a 'scandal.'" While they suggest that this supports the conspiracy theory, in fact the scandal in the quotation is the delay in publication. Finally, it is hard to imagine what they think the scrolls can contain that would overthrow or even seriously threaten Christianity. In a worst-case scenario, there might be a document that reads like this: "Dear Jesus, How's everything in Rome? Here at Qumran we're still laughing about that fake crucifixion stunt. Best regards to Mary Magdalene and the kids. Your cousin, John." Would a find like this prove that Barbara Thiering is correct? Or would the document be dismissed as an outrageous hoax in very poor taste?

It is significant to note that while Baigent and Leigh maintain that there is a conspiracy to distance the scrolls from Christianity, respected experts complain that the scrolls have been tied too closely to it. In *Reclaiming the Dead Sea Scrolls*, Lawrence H. Schiffman, a member of the expanded editorial team, argues that the members of the original International Team "attempted all too much to describe the material in Christian terms, never really confronting the Jewish character of the [scrolls]."

Rather than a conspiracy, however, Schiffman sees an unfortunate sequence of events. It will be remembered that the first scrolls were discovered just as Palestine erupted into open warfare between Jews and Arabs. Four of the scrolls ended up in Jordanian-controlled East Jerusalem, in the hands of Christians who either were openly hostile to or at best unsympathetic toward Israel. Among these scrolls was the rule book of a hermit-like brotherhood similar to the Essenes. Because the Qumran region was occupied by Jordan, the thousands of fragments unearthed in the search of Caves 2-11 were studied at the École Biblique in East Jerusalem, where no Jews could see them—not even Jews from France, England, or America. Thus, says Schiffman, each new text was fitted into a theory that focused on how the Essenes were the earlier version of Christianity, preparing the way in the wilderness, so to speak. In the meantime, Jews who might have been interested in the legal documents, and were competent enough to interpret them, were excluded.

Schiffman is certainly correct in claiming that people see what they are trained to see. The rule book among the first scrolls received the title *Manual of Discipline* because Millar Burrows, the director of the American Schools, was reminded of a Methodist "Discipline." The Essenes are called monks, and Qumran is described as a monastery with a baptistry, refectory, and scriptorium because these words are familiar to Christian writers. A Jew looking at the same site sees a *mikveh* (a pool for ritual bathing), dining room, and a *shul* (a place of study). Schiffman also is extremely kind in his description of the original editors. But others, including Christians, have commented on the anti-Semitism of John Allegro and John Strugnell, and the offensive, if not anti-Semitic, remarks of Millar Burrows and John Trever. In the fall of 1990, Strugnell made disrespectful statements about Judaism in an interview with an Israeli newspaper and was removed as editor of the International Team. And, as noted earlier, in reviewing the events surrounding Yigael Yadin's purchase of Mar Samuel's scrolls, John Trever told Neil Asher Silberman, "I was trying to find a way that would keep it out of the control of the Jews." It seems fair to wonder whether the religious views of these scholars influenced their work on the scrolls, which are, after all, Jewish texts.

For his part, Robert Eisenman believes that because Jewish scrolls experts are unfamiliar with New Testament scholarship, they have adopted the incorrect Christian agreement about Qumran. He maintains that the Romans executed Jesus as a Jewish revolutionary, a Zealot. James the Just, the

Teacher of Righteousness, continued as leader of the movement but was betrayed by Paul, the Man of Lies. Since Paul
won out over James, the four accepted Gospels, which are
consistent with Paul's understanding of Jesus, created a false
cover story in which "the Jews" reject Jesus and have him executed. As Eisenman explained in an interview with Silberman,
those who accept the Essene authorship of the scrolls leave the
Gospel account unchallenged, thereby "confirming the
Christian accusations against the Jewish people, and...not
allowing our people to get out from under these terrible blood
libels [lies]...."

The scrolls, therefore, demand a revision of outdated
views about Judaism and Christianity. Jews will find that
Christianity shares more with their religion than they had
imagined. And Christians will have to throw out some traditional beliefs about Judaism. The challenge comes from the
existence of the scrolls themselves, quite apart from what they
say. The well-worn argument that Judaism had become nothing more than a group of laws is denied by the very fact that
the scrolls existed. Regardless of how close their ideas were to
those of Jesus, Jewish poets were composing hymns, scholars
were writing biblical commentaries, theologians were describing the end of time, and professional secretaries were making
multiple copies for libraries. All this happened at a time and
place that some later Christians have described as a dull, unin-
teresting period. Historians may have to correct incorrect
views, and anti-Semites may be disturbed by what the scrolls
reveal, but they are not a threat to Christianity. Respected
New Testament scholarship today is concerned with placing
Jesus in this Jewish time and place and in finding the true

connections between Judaism and early Christianity. At this level, at least, there is no conspiracy.

CHAPTER 10

How the Scrolls Changed History

The expression "to change history" can aptly be applied to two different circumstances. An event can change history if it changes the future. And historians can change history by offering a new interpretation of the past. Those who did not believe in organized religion, like Edmund Wilson and John Allegro, hoped that the Dead Sea Scrolls would change the future by weakening Christianity. Christianity, however, shows no signs of fading because of the scrolls. On the other hand, the scrolls have certainly changed our understanding of the past by providing information about the era of the Second Temple, a little-known period of great significance for Judaism, Christianity, and, ultimately, the world.

Before the discovery of the scrolls, few Jewish documents existed from the centuries immediately before the rise of Christianity, and almost nothing existed in the Hebrew and Aramaic languages. What did exist in Greek—books of the Apocrypha like Ben Sira and Maccabees, and others like the Wisdom of Solomon and Jubilees—survived because groups within Judaism or Christianity considered them valuable and continually made copies. These documents, created for a Greek-influenced readership, therefore offer a limited or edited glimpse of what was thought and believed. Likewise, the picture of Judaism in the New Testament includes only what is background to the main story—the mission of Jesus. People appear as villains or heroes in terms of this focus; beliefs and practices are commonly mentioned only when Jesus opposes them. A reader of the New Testament gets the impression that the message of Jesus emerges out of nowhere, that it has no history of its own, that it is new and unique. This, in fact, is the view that many Church historians took and that Church leaders were happy to teach.

Wilson and Allegro considered this to be a central idea of Christianity. If this support were removed, if Christianity were shown to be merely one stage in religious thought, then, they believed, the entire religion would collapse. The Dead Sea Scrolls have changed history by showing how the ideas of Jesus and the early Church were based on Jewish beliefs. Far from weakening Christianity, however, this has supported its claim to being a true offspring of the religion of Israel.

Some of the supposed connections between Christianity and the Dead Sea sect have been overstated. One is that Christians lived at Qumran before its destruction by the Romans. Jesus Christ traveled and preached, but there is no record of his having written anything. Yet the Gospels contain accounts of his sermons, public speeches, and private conversations. Possibly, some of his followers kept a record of his activities and wrote down his words. Likewise, people who saw him in action may have shared stories with friends and neighbors, repeating as best they could what they had heard. In this way, written and oral traditions circulated among those who were attracted to what scholars have called the Jesus movement, the early beginnings of Christianity. Later, some of these traditions were collected and edited into the Gospels. New Testament experts disagree about when this occurred and about the historical value of the traditions. Some believe that the author of John was one of the apostles, John the son of Zebedee, and that other Gospel authors may have known Jesus or his disciples. Others argue that even the earliest Gospel was written a generation after Jesus's death, and whatever eyewitness accounts may have existed were heavily edited and turned into stories to demonstrate specific points.

The possibility that the Dead Sea Scrolls might mention Jesus or his disciples therefore proved exciting to many people. Now we know that the names Jesus, Paul, and John the Baptist do not appear in any of the published scrolls. But, admittedly, few actual historical persons are named, since the characters are given titles: Teacher of Righteousness, Wicked Priest, Man of Lies. Barbara Thiering argued that the Gospels were written in this same coded style by the sect that wrote the biblical commentaries, the *pesharim*, among the Dead Sea Scrolls. Robert Eisenman associated the Qumran sect with the church of James the Just, whom he identifies as the Teacher of Righteousness. Galatians 2:12 indicates that James, brother of Jesus, disagreed with Paul about the need for followers of Jesus to observe Jewish ritual law. And the Epistle of James (2:17) makes the same point: "Faith without works is dead." Even more extreme, the letter states (2:10): "Whoever keeps the whole law except for one point is guilty of breaking all of it."

Eisenman finds views like these typical of the Teacher of Righteousness. He also sees in the *Habakkuk Commentary* a dispute between the Teacher and the Man of Lies over strict observance of the law. In his view, since Paul preached salvation by faith and denounced the burden of the law, he is the Man of Lies. Christianity, which has been shaped by Paul's epistles, therefore began as a deliberate changing of Jewish emphasis on law. These views, however, have few supporters among scrolls scholars, although Thiering's claim was featured in a television documentary, "Riddle of the Dead Sea Scrolls," and Eisenman's is central to the conspiracy theory in *The Dead Sea Scrolls Deception* by Michael Baigent and Richard Leigh.

In 1972, Father José O'Callaghan claimed that three tiny papyrus fragments from Cave 7—7Q5—contained passages from the Gospel of Mark. He also claimed to have identified fragments of Greek papyri with verses from Acts, Romans, James, 1 Timothy, and 2 Peter. Qumran was destroyed by the Romans in about 68 A.D. If these claims could be proven, and if the Cave 7 fragments, which are all in Greek, belonged to Qumran, an early dating of the New Testament would also be proven. This would increase the historical believability of the Gospel narratives and quotations. Such an idea thrilled conservative Christians who reject the liberal view that the Gospels were composed late in the first century. An early date also might help prove that the epistles of Peter were written by Peter the apostle, not by one or two different Peters at the end of the first or well into the second century.

It might prove, too, that other New Testament authors were Jewish Christians in the Holy Land, not Gentile Christians in Rome and elsewhere. O'Callaghan's crediting of 7Q5 to Mark was supported by a few scholars, most recently Carsten Thiede in *The Earliest Gospel Manuscript?* But they do not all agree that the Cave 7 find, which is so different from the others, belonged to the Qumran residents driven out by Romans. If Christians came to Qumran after 68 A.D., their scrolls would be unimportant in dating the New Testament.

Moreover, most Bible experts do not find the reconstructions convincing. The disputed passage in 7Q5 is from Mark 6:52-53, which in English translation reads: "For they did not understand about the loaves, for their hearts were hardened. And when they had passed over, they came to the land of Gennesaret and drew to shore." The Greek fragment—a scrap about $1^1/_2$ by 1 inch, or the size of a postage stamp—contains twenty letters or traces of letters on five lines. Only ten of the letters are clearly identifiable. Only one word is complete— *kai*, or "and." The other words are reconstructed from as few as one letter or trace, distributed at irregular intervals among the lines. If the width of the column were known, a papyrus expert like O'Callaghan could make a reconstruction from such thin evidence by determining the number of missing letters and spaces. But O'Callaghan's reconstruction assumes that the scribe made a spelling error; and still it does not agree with the standard Greek text or any known variation. Most New Testament experts, even conservatives who wish he were right, feel that O'Callaghan is asking too much. One scholar, C. H. Roberts of Oxford, even joked that *he* could make that fragment part of any Greek text he chose.

The most likely connections between the scrolls and Christianity are those that show parallels in ritual, language, beliefs, and biblical interpretation. Parallels might show that Jesus and other New Testament figures borrowed ideas from the Qumran sect. Or they may have resulted because Christianity and the Qumran sect descended from the same kind of Judaism, or because these ideas were circulating among Jews at the time and were available to everyone. The twelve apostles parallel the Qumran sect's Council of Twelve, but they also both are similar to the twelve tribes of Israel and the twelve signs of the zodiac. The *pesher* method of interpreting the Bible to reflect current events is similar to the way the Gospel authors portray Jesus fulfilling previous prophesies, but this technique also is found in rabbinic commentaries. So, too, ritual bathing, communal meals, and shared property are common to Qumran and the New Testament. Ritual bathing was practiced by the Sadducees and Pharisees as well, although probably not as frequently as at Qumran. If later sources are correct, the Sadducees and Pharisees did not hold property in common. But if we knew more about other sects, we might discover that these practices were widespread.

Nonetheless, the lifestyle of the Qumran sectarians immediately reminds us of John the Baptist, especially the ritual bathing, or baptism. John preached a "baptism of repentance for the forgiveness of sins" (Mark 1:4; Luke 3:3). The *Manual of Discipline* (column 3, lines 3-9) says that whoever rejects the laws of God cannot be cleansed by waters of ablution (holy waters), but whoever accepts them is cleansed by water. Both John and the Qumran sect practiced this extreme form of purity because they believed that the final judgment—the "day of the Lord"—was at hand. In addition, the Qumran sect was led by a priest, renounced worldly wealth, lived simply, and moved to the wilderness to avoid corruption and impurity.

According to the Gospel of Luke, John was of a priestly family. He lived in the wilderness and may have ministered in the area north of Qumran. Moreover, the language that the Gospels use in discussing John resembles the language of the scrolls. The *Manual of Discipline* (8:13-15) explains that the group moved to the wilderness in accordance with the prophecy (Isaiah 40:3): "In the wilderness prepare the way of the Lord." John is described as "the voice of one crying in the wilderness, Prepare the way of the Lord" (Mark 1:3). The *Manual* (8:6-10) refers to the community of the chosen as the true Temple of the Lord, the source of atonement, "the precious cornerstone whose foundation can not be shaken." John says, "God is able to raise up children to Abraham from these stones" (Matthew 3:9). Experts have noted that since in Hebrew *banim* is "children" and *'abanim* is "stones," John may have been pointing to those he was baptizing, not to actual stones, and calling them the true Temple.

Despite these similarities, there are many differences between John and the Qumran sect. John the Baptist is never called an Essene in the New Testament or by the Jewish historian Josephus, who describes his career. While the Essenes turned their backs on the world and concentrated on preparing themselves for the final day, John preached to the masses. And while John, like the Qumran sect, lived in the wilderness, those he baptized returned to their homes. Some experts, however, believe that John the Baptist was at one time an Essene or that he studied among the Qumran sect. His father was a priest at the Temple in Jerusalem, but Luke (1:80) says that as a child John lived in the wilderness. Since Qumran is only a few miles from Jerusalem, it has been suggested that perhaps John was "adopted" by the Essenes, who, according to Josephus, accepted young boys for training. Clearly, John's later ministry marks him as different from the Essenes, but the similarities between his thought and practice and that of the Essenes are noteworthy.

There also are striking similarities between the language of the scrolls and that of the New Testament. Before the discovery of the scrolls, Hebrew and Aramaic documents from the immediate pre-Christian era were almost nonexistent. This led some Bible experts to conclude that Jews were not composing literature at the time or were not writing in their simple and rough native language. Whether this native language was Hebrew or Aramaic was also a matter of debate among most Christian scholars, who finally believed the native language was Aramaic and labeled the later Hebrew of the Mishnah (the Jewish law code) an artificial literary language. But whether Jesus was preaching in Hebrew or Aramaic, the Gospels record his words in Greek translation. And translation always involves the risk of being influenced by the person who makes the translation—his culture and times. For example, as we have already seen, the Essenes may have led lives of poverty in a communal settlement, but to call them monks in a monastery is to use words that did not even exist in their time. Thus, New Testament scholars need to know whether Greek phrasing has changed the true words of Jesus. The scrolls provide something of an answer.

First, the scrolls are evidence that Hebrew and Aramaic were living languages at the time of Jesus. They contain original hymns, prayers, legal documents, and sect records. In addition, some of the works, like the *Copper Scroll,* use a simple, nonliterary language, while the spelling in others reflects the pronunciation of actual spoken words. This lends support to conservative Bible scholars who argue that Mary, a Jewish woman speaking Hebrew or Aramaic, would have been capable of composing the "Magnificat," the hymn recorded in Luke 1:46-55, beginning "My soul magnifies the Lord, my spirit rejoices in God my savior." Experts who believe that Hebrew and Aramaic were simple languages unsuitable for writing argue that a later author composed the hymn in Greek and an editor put it into Mary's mouth.

Second, phrases that are familiar from the Greek of the New Testament appear in the scrolls in their original forms. Perhaps the most significant phrase is *mashiah*, "anointed one," which is translated in English as "Messiah." In the Hebrew Bible a person appointed to special office was often sprinkled or anointed with oil. This could be a priest, a prophet, or a king; the king of Judah of the Davidic dynasty was "the Lord's anointed."

In the post-biblical period, Jews looked forward to the arrival of an anointed leader who would save them from the Romans. The Qumran scrolls speak of two Messiahs who will lead the community: the secular (or lay) Messiah of Israel and the priestly Messiah of Aaron. The New Testament, of course, focuses on one Messiah, using the Greek translation for "anointed one"—Christ. The scrolls also speak of a *mebaqqer*, or "overseer," who supervises the new members of the sect and acts as teacher and role model. The Greek translation of this word is *episkopos*, from *epi*, "over," plus *skop*, "look." It was translated into Latin as *episcopos* or *(e)biscop(us)*, from which it came into English as "bishop." Other important New Testament words and phrases that appear in their original form in the scrolls are *power, mystery, poor in spirit, sons of light, works of the law, righteousness of God,* and *church of God.*

In addition to words and phrases, the New Testament also contains whole passages or groups of ideas that appear in the Dead Sea Scrolls. One striking example is the Qumran sect's central belief in the eternal conflict between Light and Darkness, understood in Jewish terms as the forces of good and evil (as distinct from the Zoroastrian belief in two opposing cosmic beings, or gods).

In a well-known passage in 2 Corinthians 6:14-16, Paul uses the literary device of opposites to capture this spiritual doubleness: "Do not be yoked with unbelievers; for what do righteousness and unrighteousness have in common, or what fellowship does light have with darkness? What agreement can Christ have with Beliar? What does a believer have in common with an unbeliever? What agreement does the temple of God have with idols? For you are the temple of the living God." Like the Qumran texts, this passage tells the faithful to separate from unbelievers because Light has nothing to do with Darkness. The name Beliar, which occurs only here in the New Testament, is also interesting. It is probably a variant (or misspelling) of Belial, which appears in the Dead Sea Scrolls as the name of the leader of Evil.

The "beatitudes"—lists of behavior beginning with the formula "Blessed is…"—provide another interesting literary parallel between the New Testament and the scrolls. Quite a few psalms contain this opening, 'ashre in Hebrew, most often in single sentences. Psalm 1:1 opens with "Blessed is the man that walks not in the counsel of the ungodly." Psalm 2 ends: "Blessed are all who put their trust in him." A number of psalms couple such verses. The opening two verses of Psalm 119 are: "Blessed are they whose path is undefiled, who walk in the law of the Lord. Blessed are they who keep his testimonies, who seek him with their whole heart."

To readers of the New Testament, the most familiar list is in the Sermon on the Mount: "Blessed are the poor in spirit, for theirs is the kingdom of heaven. Blessed are they who mourn, for they shall be comforted. Blessed are the meek, for they shall inherit the earth" (Matthew 5:1-3). Now we have the Dead Sea document 4Q525, which, although incomplete, clearly contains a series of sentences that begin with 'ashre. Emile Puech reads part of the document as: "Blessed are those who cling to his statutes and who do not cling to her ways of perversity. Blessed are those who rejoice because of her and who do not spread themselves in the ways of folly.... Blessed is the man who has attained Wisdom and walks in the law of the Most High...."

A final example of a parallel use of words is the use of the formula "You say.... I say...." In the Sermon on the Mount, Jesus says, "You have heard it said by them of old.... But I say to you" (Matthew 5: 21-45). In the *Halakhic Letter,* also called *Miqṣat Maʿase ha-Torah,* the disagreements between the Qumran sect and its opponents are introduced by the formula "We think.... You know...."

In terms of beliefs, besides the opposites of Light and Darkness, the Dead Sea Scrolls and the New Testament share a belief that the final judgment is near and the chosen will be saved by an anointed one, a Messiah. The scrolls speak of two future leaders, one religious, one secular, called the Messiah of Aaron and the Messiah of Israel, the latter being also the "branch of David." In the New Testament, both of these offices are combined in Jesus. The genealogies (a list that shows who a person is descended from) in Matthew 1 and Luke 3 trace Jesus's ancestry to King David; in Revelation 5:5, Jesus is called the "root of David." And in Hebrews he is said to be "high priest forever after the order of Melchizedek" (5:6, 6:20). In addition, a scroll fragment contains fascinating phrasing related to this. In Luke 1 (31-32, 35), an angel tells Mary: "You shall conceive in your womb and bear a son and name him Jesus. He shall be great and shall be called the Son of the Most High. And the Lord God shall give to him the throne of his forefather David...[and he] shall be called the Son of God."

In the Hebrew Bible, the Davidic king is often called the son of God. For instance, in 2 Samuel 7 the prophet Nathan has a vision in which God tells him to assure King David that after his death his son "will build a house for my name, and I will establish the throne of his kingdom forever. I will be his father, and he will be my son" (13-14). While this clearly refers to a human son and an earthly kingdom, by the time of the Dead Sea Scrolls, the phrase "son of God" had taken on the hint that a Messiah would come. The text known as the *Florilegium* (4Q174) interprets this passage as follows: "This refers to the branch of David who will arise with the Interpreter of the Law...in the last days." And in an Aramaic fragment (4Q246) we find: "He will be called Son of God and they will name him Son of the Most High." These terms and their hints at a Messiah were later applied to Jesus.

Finally, as we have seen, both the Qumran texts and the New Testament treat the Hebrew Bible as a source to be borrowed from for its own purposes. To a modern reader, this approach can seem nonsensical. How can isolated sentences be yanked from their original position in a text and be made to mean something entirely unrelated? How could people believe that the speeches of Isaiah or the words of the Psalms, for example, were not understood by their immediate audience, only to be understood in hindsight by those who lived many years later? Yet this is what is implied by the proof-texts in the Gospels—those passages that refer to Jesus doing something to fulfill a prophesy in the Old Testament. Thus, Jesus lived in Capernaum, by the sea near the territory of Zebulun and Naphtali, "to fulfill that which was spoken by the prophet Isaiah, Land of Zebulun and land of Naphthali, on the way to the sea, beyond Jordan, Galilee of the Gentiles—the people who sit in darkness have seen a great light" (Matthew 4:14-16). So, too, Jesus speaks in parables "to fulfill that which was spoken by the prophet, I will open my mouth in parables, I will utter things which have been kept secret since the foundation of the world" (Matthew 13:35, rewording Psalm 78:2).

As forced as this technique may seem, it was not invented by the authors of the Gospels. It is central to the biblical commentaries of the Qumran scrolls, which take verses from the Bible and apply them to the history of the sect and to the end of time. Thus the *Florilegium* interprets 2 Samuel 7:11—"I will give you rest from all your enemies"—as meaning "he will give them rest from the sons of Belial...they come with the plan of Belial to make the sons of light stumble...."

Obviously, these similarities do not cancel out the many differences between the Qumran sect and Christianity. At no point do the Dead Sea Scrolls suggest that the Teacher of Righteousness is divine or the object of worship. Nor do they find a saving grace in his death or expect his resurrection. The sect strictly observed Jewish ritual in preparation for the appearance of the Messiahs who would bring in the final days. The New Testament, in contrast, focuses on salvation through the death of Jesus, a Messiah who has already appeared and will return. Nevertheless, the scrolls have rewritten the history of early Christianity. Some Church experts have long argued two essentially contradictory positions: first, that the ministry of Jesus was an original and unique revelation and second that Christianity is the true religion of Israel. The scrolls have shaken the first argument by placing the Jesus movement in its Jewish context. But the scrolls have given new life to the second position by showing that Christianity can claim an authentic Jewish heritage.

CONCLUSION

The Book of Mysteries

> They know not the mystery to come,
> Nor do they understand the things of the past.
> They know not that which shall befall them,
> Nor do they save their soul from the mystery to come.

These words from The Book of Mysteries (1Q27) capture much of the Qumran sect's philosophy. In the final days, the "day of the Lord," only those who know the mysteries or secrets of the Bible will be saved. And only the chosen sons of Zadok, the Sons of Light, know these mysteries.

In a non-religious version, this is also the view of many modern thinkers. Historians, of course, do not need to make up good reasons for what they do. Learning about the past is a perfectly valid goal in and of itself. The Dead Sea Scrolls are valuable, like Egyptian hieroglyphics or Native American drawings, because they fill in the story of civilization, the drama of human existence. Nonetheless, many people feel that everything must have a practical application. History is worth studying, they say, because the past teaches us about the present and because understanding the errors of our ancestors allows us to make a better future. As the American philosopher George Santayana said: "Those who cannot remember the past are condemned to repeat it."

One of the strange things about professional and popular interest surrounding the Dead Sea Scrolls is that people of widely differing views believe that the scrolls contain just the evidence they need to prove their particular views.

Early excitement among conservative Christians stemmed from the hope that something in the scrolls would prove the Gospel story. Time and again, the non-believer John Allegro said that when made public this or that scroll would cause the collapse of Christianity. Edmund Wilson hoped that the scrolls would weaken the mythology of Christianity. Yet despite the bitter arguments that have captured so many headlines, any number of people agree in hoping that the message of the scrolls will lead to greater peace and harmony. Allegro sought permission from the Jordanian government to establish a center in East Jerusalem that would bring together scrolls experts of all nationalities and religions—except, presumably, Jews. Robert Eisenman has argued that the scrolls reveal the Jewishness of true Christianity and, therefore, have the power to eliminate anti-Semitism. And Lawrence Schiffman believes that by showing Christianity's deep roots in Judaism, the scrolls will promote mutual respect among believers in the two great religions.

Yet, there is cause for doubt and pessimism. As The Book of Mysteries observes:

> What people would wish to be oppressed by another more powerful than itself?
> Who would wish to be sinfully looted of its wealth?
> And yet, which is the people not to oppress its neighbor?
> Where is the people which has not looted another of its wealth?

The saga of the Dead Sea Scrolls offers ample evidence of both forgivable and unforgivable behavior on the part of those involved. Those who toil in the vineyard of the Lord do not expect material wealth. And those who toil in the university work in places that cherish the names of rich industrialists and railroad tycoons. They seek their own immortality by writing books that future generations will read or by promoting ideas that other ages will remember. It is easy to forgive the eagerness to have one's name associated with the Dead Sea Scrolls, especially with a first edition of an important text. But other offenses seem inexcusable and mean-spirited. The Jordanian government, which had occupied the territory of the proposed Palestinian state in the British Mandate, claimed ownership of the Temple Scroll at a meeting of UNESCO in 1969.

And in 1994 Palestinian authorities laid claim to all the Qumran scrolls that had been found in areas they hoped would one day become part of their sovereign state. Are these Muslim governments seriously interested in supporting research into Jewish and Christian origins?

Yet there are those who find hope even in the failures and missteps of the scrolls saga. James VanderKam sees something positive emerging from the scandalous delay in publication: both the Society of Biblical Literature and the American Schools of Oriental Research now have policy statements supporting the principle that discoveries must be made available quickly. And Edward Cook feels that the debates over the meaning and significance of the scrolls emphasize how uncertain our knowledge of the past really is. While few experts would have expected that after fifty years so many questions would remain unanswered, a little humility is not a bad thing.

Whether or not the Dead Sea Scrolls will be the vehicle that brings about a Golden Age, we can still look forward to a time when, in the words of The Book of Mysteries:

> ... wickedness shall be banished by righteousness
>
> as darkness is banished by light.
>
> As smoke clears and is no more
>
> so shall wickedness perish for ever
>
> and righteousness be revealed like a sun.

BIBLIOGRAPHY

I. TEXTS

Charlesworth, James H., ed. *The Dead Sea Scrolls: Hebrew, Aramaic, and Greek Texts with English Translations.* Louisville, Ky.: Westminster John Knox Press, 1994.

Eisenman, Robert H., and James M. Robinson, eds. *A Facsimile Edition of the Dead Sea Scrolls.* Washington, D.C.: Biblical Archaeology Society, 1991.

Eisenman, Robert H., and Michael Wise, eds. *Dead Sea Scrolls Uncovered.* Harmondsworth, England: Penguin Books, 1992.

García Martínez, Florentino. *The Dead Sea Scrolls Translated: The Qumran Texts in English.* Leiden: Brill, 1994.

Gaster, Theodor H. *The Dead Sea Scriptures.* 3rd ed. New York: Anchor Books, 1976.

Vermes, Geza. *The Complete Dead Sea Scrolls in English.* Harmondsworth, England: Allen Lane, 1997.

Wacholder, Ben Zion, and Martin G. Abegg, eds. *A Preliminary Edition of the Unpublished Dead Sea Scrolls.* Washington, D.C.: Biblical Archaeology Society, 1991-96.

Wise, Michael, Martin Abegg, Jr., and Edward Cook, eds. *The Dead Sea Scrolls.* San Francisco: HarperSanFrancisco, 1996.

II. STUDIES

Allegro, John M.

> 1960 *The Treasure of the Copper Scroll.*
> Garden City, N.Y.: Doubleday.

> 1971 *The Dead Sea Scrolls: A Reappraisal.*
> Harmondsworth, England: Penguin Books.

Baigent, Michael, and Richard Leigh. *The Dead Sea Scrolls Deception.* London: Jonathan Cape, 1991.

Baron, Salo Wittmayer. *A Social and Religious History of the Jews.* Vol. II, 2d ed. New York: Columbia University Press, 1952.

Brandon, S.G.F. *Jesus and the Zealots.* New York: Charles Scribner's Sons, 1967.

Burrows, Millar. *The Dead Sea Scrolls.* New York: Viking, 1956.

Charlesworth, James H., ed. *John and the Dead Sea Scrolls.* New York: Crossroad, 1990.

Collins, John J. "A Pre-Christian 'Son of God' Among the Dead Sea Scrolls," *Bible Review* 9:3 (June 1993), 34-38, 57.

Cook, Edward M.

> 1994 *Solving the Mysteries of the Dead Sea Scrolls.*
> Grand Rapids: Zondervan.

> 1996 (November-December) "What Was Qumran?— A Ritual Purification Center," *Biblical Archaeology Review* 22:6, 39, 48-51, 73-75.

Cross, Frank M. *The Ancient Library of Qumran and Modern Biblical Studies.* Grand Rapids: Baker Book House, 1980.

Crown, Alan D., and Lena Cansdale. "Qumran: Was It an Essene Settlement?" *Biblical Archaeology Review* 20:5 (September/October 1994), 25-35, 73-78.

Davies, A. Powell. *The Meaning of the Dead Sea Scrolls.* New York: New American Library, 1956.

Durant, Will. *Caesar and Christ. The Story of Civilization.* Vol. III. New York: Simon and Schuster, 1944.

Eisenman, Robert.

1983 *Maccabees, Zadokites, Christians and Qumran.* Leiden: Brill.

1986 *James the Just in the Habakkuk Pesher.* Leiden: Brill.

Goshen-Gottstein, Moshe H.

1967 "Hebrew Biblical Manuscripts: Their History and Their Place in the HUBP Edition," *Biblica* 48, 243-89.

1979 "The Aleppo Codex and the Rise of the Masoretic Bible Text," *Biblical Archaeologist* 42:3, 145-63.

Greenberg, Moshe. *Studies in the Bible and Jewish Thought.* Philadelphia: Jewish Publication Society, 1995.

Lehmann, Manfred. "Where the Temple Tax Was Buried," *Biblical Archaeology Review* 19:6 (November/December 1993), 38-43.

Magnes, Jodi. "What Was Qumran?—Not a Country Villa," *Biblical Archaeology Review* 22:6 (November/December 1996), 38, 40-47, 72-73.

Minkoff, Harvey. *Approaches to the Bible.* 2 vols. Washington, D.C.: Biblical Archaeology Society, 1994-95.

Propp, William Henry, Baruch Halpern, and David Noel
Freedman, eds. *The Hebrew Bible and Its
Interpreters.* Winona Lake, Ind.: Eisenbrauns, 1990.

Raban, Avner, and Robert R. Stieglitz. "The Sea People and
Their Contributions to Civilization," *Biblical
Archaeology Review* 17:6 (November/December 1991),
34-42.

Scanlin, Harold. *The Dead Sea Scrolls and Modern Translations
of the Old Testament.* Wheaton, Il.: Tyndale House, 1993.

Schiffman, Lawrence H.

1991 *From Text to Tradition: A History of Second
Temple and Rabbinic Judaism.* Hoboken,
N.J.: Ktav.

1994 *Reclaiming the Dead Sea Scrolls.*
Philadelphia: Jewish Publication Society.

Schürer, Emil. *A History of the Jewish People in the Time of
Jesus.* English translation, 1886-1890. New York:
Schocken, 1961.

Shanks, Hershel.

1984 (September-October) "Yigael Yadin, 1917-
1984." *Biblical Archaeology Review* 10:5, 24-29.

1993 (May-June) "The Qumran Settlement:
Monastery, Villa or Fortress?" *Biblical
Archaeology Review* 19:3, 62-65.

1994 (March-April) "Peace, Politics and
Archaeology," *Biblical Archaeology Review*
20:2, 50-57, 94.

Shanks, Hershel, et al. *The Dead Sea Scrolls After Forty Years.*
Washington, D.C.: Biblical Archaeology Society, 1991.

Shanks, Hershel, ed. *Understanding the Dead Sea Scrolls*. New York: Random House, 1992.

Silberman, Neil Asher. *The Hidden Scrolls*. New York: Riverhead Books, 1994.

Stanton, Graham. "A Gospel among the Scrolls?" *Bible Review* 11:6 (December 1995), 36-42.

Thied, Carsten. *The Earliest Gospel Manuscript? The Qumran Fragment 7Q5 and Its Significance for New Testament Studies*. Exeter: Paternoster, 1992.

Thiering, Barbara. *Jesus and the Riddle of the Dead Sea Scrolls*. San Francisco: HarperSanFrancisco, 1992.

Trever, John C. *The Dead Sea Scrolls: A Personal Account*. Grand Rapids: Eerdmans, 1977.

VanderKam, James C. *The Dead Sea Scrolls Today*. Grand Rapids: Eerdmans, 1994.

Viviano, Benedict T. "Beatitudes Found among Dead Sea Scrolls," *Biblical Archaeology Review* 18:6 (November/December 1992), 53-55, 66.

Wilson, Edmund. *Israel and the Dead Sea Scrolls*. New York: Farrar Strauss Giroux, 1969.

Woude, Adam S. van der. "Tracing the Evolution of the Hebrew Bible," *Bible Review* 11:1 (February 1995), 42-45.

Yadin, Yigael.

1966 *Masada*. New York: Random House.

1971 *Bar-Kokhba*. Jerusalem: Weidenfeld and Nicolson.

1985 *The Temple Scroll: The Hidden Law of the Dead Sea Sect*. New York: Random House.

ABOUT THE AUTHOR

Harvey Minkoff, Ph.D., is professor of English Linguistics at Hunter College of the City University of New York. A specialist in Bible translation who works with Hebrew, Aramaic, Greek, and Latin, he has published many articles about the language and literary structure of the Bible. Recently, he edited a two-volume work entitled *Approaches to the Bible.*

NOTES

NOTES